THE DANCING MASTER

THE
DANCING
MASTER

BY

P. RAMEAU

*Dancing-Master to the Pages of Her
Catholic Majesty the Queen of Spain*

TRANSLATED BY

CYRIL W. BEAUMONT

*From the Original Edition published at
Paris, 1725, & Embellished with 57 Plates*

ALTON
Dance Books
2003

First published in 1931 by C. W. Beaumont
This facsimile edition published in 2003 by Dance Books Ltd.,
The Old Bakery, 4 Lenten Street, Alton, Hampshire GU34 1HG
www.dancebooks.co.uk

Copyright © 2003 Imperial Society of Teachers of Dancing

ISBN 1 85273 092 7

Printed by Russell Press, Nottingham

This *English* Translation of P. RAMEAU's
Maître à Danser is affectionately Inscribed

To MARGARET CRASKE

As a little gesture of friendship

from

THE TRANSLATOR

INTRODUCTION

RAMEAU'S *Maître à Danser* is the standard work on the technique of eighteenth century dancing. It was first issued at Paris in 1725, dedicated to the Duc de Retz and bearing the printed approbation of the celebrated dancer and *maître de ballet*, Louis Pécourt. It may be of interest to cite this in an English rendering: "I have read, by order of the Keeper of the Seals, a Manuscript bearing the title *Le Maître à Danser*, &c. I have found in this work all the precepts of dancing set forth precisely and clearly. The engraved plates which represent the various postures of the body will render the execution easier and I believe that this book will be of no less service to the student desirous of learning dancing, than it will lighten the labours of those who teach it." This edition contains a frontispiece, four folding plates and fifty-four full-page plates, all engraved by the author. The drawing of these is somewhat naïve, but the meaning is plain.

Of Rameau himself, who must not be confused with the composer Jean Philippe Rameau (1683–1764), I can discover nothing but what he himself tells us on the title-page—that he was "*Maître à Danser des Pages de Sa Majesté Catholique la Reine d'Espagne.*" Towards the end of the year 1725—the *privilege* is dated November 8th—he published a second book, entitled *Abbrégé de la Nouvelle Methode dans l'Art d'Ecrire ou de Tracer toutes sortes de Danses de Ville*. This is a treatise on dance notation, a simplification and improved version of Feuillet's *Chorégraphie* (1701). On the title-page of this book, Rameau is described as "*Maître à Danser Ordinaire de la Maison de Sa Majesté Catholique, la Reine seconde Douairrière d'Espagne*; which proves that he was dancing-master to Elizabeth Farnese (1692–1766), the only daughter of Odoardo II, Prince of

Parma, who, in 1714, became the second wife of Philip V of Spain.

As a guide to contemporary social etiquette in the ballroom, the dances that were in vogue, the different kinds of honours that were paid, the various steps and arm movements in use and how they were executed, the *Maître à Danser* is an invaluable source of information. For, although the eighteenth century witnessed the publication in France of several books on dancing which record the steps and arm movements used in certain famous contemporary dances, these do not explain how the steps are to be done. This information was first made available in the *Maître à Danser*.

At this stage, a word of caution is advisable. When the dance student meets with a familiar technical term, there is a not unnatural tendency to interpret it in the light of modern technique, with which the student is doubtless familiar. Nothing could be more fallacious or more apt to produce difficulties where none exist. The student should do no more than carry out the author's instructions, for, although many eighteenth century steps bear familiar names, as regards their manner of execution they frequently differ considerably from their modern equivalents.

Rameau's *Maître à Danser*, first published at Paris in 1725[1], by Jean Villette, "*rue Saint Jacques, à la Croix d'Or,*" was reissued in 1726. There are several later editions; one, dated 1734, being printed by Jean Villette *fils*, at the same address. The typographical arrangement of the title-page differs slightly from that of the first edition, otherwise it is obviously printed from the same type and plates.

The first English edition was issued at London in 1728, the translation being the work of John Essex, a well-known dancing-master of the period. The book could be purchased "from the author at his House in Rood-lane, Fenchurch street; and J. Brotherton, Bookseller, at the Bible in Cornhill." This edition is illustrated with sixty

---

[1] In some copies of the first issue the plates are inserted in their appropriate places in the text, in others they are grouped together at the end of the volume.

engraved plates designed by G. Alsop. These are much more elaborate in treatment than the author's drawings and, indeed, in some instances, are inclined to be affected in style.

A second edition was published in 1731, the typographical arrangement of the title-page being revised, with a slightly extended description of the contents. In addition, the page facing the title contains an English rendering of the approbation of L. Pécourt, and the approbation (dated 1731), of Mr. Labee (*L'Abbé*), Court Dancing-Master to the Royal Family. The margins, too, are reduced. In all other respects, the text and engravings are identical, the book having clearly been printed from the same type and plates.

There is, however, another issue of this second edition bearing the same date on the title-page, but possessing an almost entirely new set of plates. This issue is likewise illustrated with sixty plates, but, while the nine diagrammatic plates are retained,[1] the rest are engraved from entirely new drawings by G. Bickham, Junr. At first glance it is a little bewildering to find two different editions bearing the same date. But a careful examination of the Bickham plates with a magnifying glass reveals the fact that a few of them bear the date 1732. As the plates used in the first issue of the second edition show no signs of wear, it may be that dancing had grown more sedate, and hence the exaggerated gestures and positions represented in some of the older plates had adversely affected the sales of the book. If this were so, the most natural course for the publisher to adopt, in order to revive interest in a standard work, would be to provide it with a new set of illustrations. However that may be, the second issue of the second edition is the sheets of the first issue with fifty-one of the former plates redrawn.

The present translation has been made from the first French edition. Part I was published serially in *The Dance*

---

[1] The four plates between pp. 48 and 49, the two plates between pp. 50 and 51, and the three plates respectively facing pp. 119, 122 and 124.

Journal. The plates are reproduced from the second issue of the second English edition, which, in my opinion, are the best. Being unable to discover a complete copy of that edition, I have to thank my friend, Mr. Randolph Schwabe, for reconstructing Figs. 2 and 16.

I take a certain pride in the publication of this volume, because it marks the attainment of a self-imposed task which I set myself in 1923—the provision for the use of British students of a small series of classical works on dancing which hitherto had not been available in an English translation, or which had become so rare as to be almost unobtainable and then only at a price prohibitive to the average pupil.

If my works on modern technique be added, the whole series affords an authentic guide to classic dance technique from the sixteenth century to the present day. As it is possible that some readers may be interested to know what is contained in the series, that shall constitute my apology for recapitulating these titles: *Orchesography*[1], by Thoinot Arbeau, 1925; *The Dancing Master*[1], by P. Rameau, 1931; *Letters on Dancing and Ballets*[1], by J. G. Noverre, 1930; *A Manual of the Theory and Practice of Classical Theatrical Dancing (Cecchetti Method)*[2], 1922; and *A Manual of the Theory and Practice of Allegro (Cecchetti Method)*[3], 1930.

In connection with the present volume, I desire to record my sincere appreciation of the kindness of Miss Margaret Craske and Miss Derra de Moroda in trying out many of the steps and in affording me much helpful criticism. I have also to thank Miss Moroda for reading through the proofs and allowing me to examine her copy of the first issue of the 1731 edition, while Miss Joan Sharp extended to me the same courtesy in regard to the copy of the 1728 edition that is contained in the Library at Cecil Sharp House. Lastly, I am much indebted to my friend, Mr. de V. Payen-Payne, who both overlooked the proofs and offered me many valuable suggestions.

CYRIL W. BEAUMONT.

[1] Translated by C. W. Beaumont.
[2] Written in collaboration with S. Idzikovsky.
[3] Written in collaboration with M. Craske.

AUTHOR'S PREFACE

IF I have called this book *The Dancing Master*, it is not because I have rashly presumed to take such a title for myself. But since, among all those who are commended for their teaching of the art of dancing, no one has been found to set down the rules governing it, I have ventured to undertake this task. Although I have spent my whole life in carefully considering the positions and balance of the body, in order to be the better fitted to impart useful lessons to my pupils, my knowledge has been acquired not so much from personal experience, as from the practices of the great masters with whom I have had the fortune to associate.

Thus I have committed to paper the lessons which they often gave in my presence. But, apart from the question as to whether or not I belong to the first rank of my profession, the rules I give will justify the title of my work.

I venture to think that my labours will not be entirely useless to those young people who, making use of this method, wish to understand and to execute more easily that which their master has taught them. For this reason I have caused many engravings to be made, showing the dancer in different positions, for rules aided by illustrations have more value than those deprived of such help.

The public will not expect from a man like myself, who has passed a lifetime in studying and teaching dancing, a long dissertation on the history, origin and antiquity of the art. I shall leave that to historians. Many celebrated authors have written on this subject, but I shall not stop to compile a list of their works.

Yet the reader would have cause to complain if, at a time when dancing has achieved the highest degree of perfection, I said nothing of the progress it had made towards the end of the last century, a progress which increases daily owing to the rivalry aroused by the performances given at the Académie Royale de Musique. For dancing must not be regarded as an exercise designed solely for pleasure. I certainly think that the joy and vivacity attendant on banquets and festivals led to its birth, but it is with dancing as with acting, men have sought to turn to useful account what was originally intended as a diversion. If dancing were confined to the theatre, it would provide occupation for a few people only; but it may be said that it merits the attention of almost everyone, even if they be destined to make use of it from their earliest years. Dancing adds graces to the gifts which nature has bestowed upon us, by regulating the movements of the body and setting it in its proper positions. And, if it do not completely eradicate the defects with which we are born, it mitigates or conceals them. This single instance will suffice to explain its utility and to excite a desire to be skilled in it.

We can say, to the glory of our race, that we have a real gift for beautiful dancing. Foreigners, so far from denying this, have, for nearly a century, come to admire our dances, and to educate themselves by our performances and in our schools. There is hardly a Court in Europe where the dancing master is not French.

The reign of Louis the Great will ever be regarded with justice as the epoch of the most illustrious men. Among all the arts which have flourished through the encouragement and liberality of so powerful a monarch, dancing has made the most rapid progress; everything has contributed to this end. That prince, endowed by nature with a noble and majestic bearing, loved from his cradle all manner of bodily exercises, and to his natural gifts added all those that can be acquired.

His passion for dancing induced him, during periods of peace, to give magnificent ballets, in which this sovereign himself did not disdain to appear with the princes and nobles of his realm. How this filled his young courtiers with emulation in the hope of being allowed to take part in the pleasures of so brilliant a Court. Nevertheless, dancing did not appear in its full glory until the birth of opera. The Italian, Lully, came to France at the age of nine to study music; endowed with a rare and sublime genius, he soon rose above all the composers of his time. Having composed the music for several ballets which I shall mention, he undertook to present to Court and Capital those lyric tragedies which still charm and arouse the admiration of the spectators. This new type of entertainment, given at the Paris theatres under the name of Opera, had hitherto been known only to the Italians.

Lully, who from his early years had been attached to the Court of Louis the Great, almost forgot his own country, and, as a result of his compositions, France easily triumphed over Italy by the charm of the very productions that had been originated at Rome and Venice. He spared no pains in according them all the splendour that music can confer. As he was obliged to represent Triumphs, Sacrifices, Enchantments and Pastorals, which required characteristic airs for their dances, he selected from all over France the most talented dancers to perform them. Beauchamps, then composer of the King's ballets, as Lully was the composer of his music, was chosen to arrange the dances for the Opéra. I cannot speak too highly of the reputation he has justly acquired. His first attempts were masterly and he always shared legitimately in the praise which the composer received in increasing measure. He was skilled and refined in his composition, and had need of capable dancers to execute what he had devised. Fortunately, he had the most skilful executants in Paris and at the Court: St. André, the elder Favier, Favre, Boutteville, Dumiraille and Germain. But, whatever the talents of all those dancers may have been, they recognized the superiority of Pécourt and L'Etang, who ever since have been the models for all those who wished to shine in the same profession. Though they differed in their characters, nature had endowed both with grace and every disposition for beautiful dancing.

L'Etang danced with nobility and precision, while Pécourt took all kinds of parts with grace, precision and lightness. Moreover, they were both well versed in the manners of polite society, so that the greatest lords delighted in their company and admitted them to their receptions.

Lully, who had lived long enough to establish his reputation, but who would have shed even greater glory on France through the new works he was engaged upon, died in 1687. At his death, Beauchamps left the Opéra. Pécourt, who had already achieved great renown as a dancer and who had even essayed his hand at devising ballets for the Court, was chosen to compose the dances for the Opéra, and he soon proved himself to be possessed of unusual talent. He had need to put forth all his powers in order to fill worthily the place of the master who had preceded him; this he accomplished by the new turns and additional graces he gave to the ballets already composed by Beauchamp.

Women, who for some time past had been permitted to take part in the ballets at the Opéra, contributed greatly to the magnificence of the spectacle. Mlles. de la Fontaine and Subligny, who distinguished themselves, aroused a spirit of emulation in many of the young *danseuses* who joined the Opéra and who were put to dance with some of the best male dancers.

Blondy, Beauchamps's nephew and worthy pupil, then came to the front and disputed honours with Ballon, whose reputation is so well founded. The latter was possessed of infinite grace and exceptional lightness. For many years he aroused the pleasure and admiration of his spectators. His talents were acknowledged by the honour conferred on him by his being permitted to be the first master to give his hand to Louis XV, our august sovereign, worshipped by his people and the patron of all arts.

Ballon having left the Opéra, lovers of dancing felt his loss. Young dancers of talent burned with a desire to fill his place.

Dumoulin, the youngest of four most talented brothers, who to-day are still distinguished for their rendering of different characters, was the one who most resembled Ballon and who consoled the public in some measure for his loss. He had the advantage at first of being associated in a *pas de deux* with Mlle. Guiot, an excellent dancer, and, by his successful efforts, made himself fitted to dance with the illustrious Mme. Prevost.

I wish I were able to pay a fitting tribute to such rare talents. All the advice which, after long meditation, we can offer in regard to our art, is contained in a single one of her dances. She puts these rules into practice with so much grace, lightness and precision, that she may well be regarded as a prodigy in her own sphere. She certainly merits the appellation of Terpsichore, the muse who presided over the dances of the ancients. She is endowed with the same power as fabled Proteus. She assumes all manner of forms at will, with the difference that, while Proteus generally employed them to frighten curious mortals who came to consult him, she makes use of them to enchant the eager eyes that watch her and to conquer all hearts. Moreover, the deserved applause accorded her aroused a noble rivalry among the other *danseuses*.

Mlle. Menese, who generally dances with Marcel in *pas de deux* of a certain style, always adds to the attraction of a performance and excites the acclamations of the public.

The beginning of Marcel's reputation is a remarkable period in the history of the Opéra.

Campra, who of all Lully's successors in musical composition has given our stage the greatest number of fine works, had just completed his *Fêtes Vénitiennes*. He had introduced into this ballet a very unusual scene, in which a dancing-master enters and sings in praise of his art, and at the same time performs all the different styles of dancing which are found in ballet. Now Marcel, who had a passable voice and a liking for singing, undertook to perform the part, which he did so well that ever afterwards the public closely watched the development of his talents for dancing, and he did not fail those who believed in him.

I may say that the *pas de deux* which he danced and still dances daily with Blondy, offer pictures so exactly related and so lively in colour, that it is impossible to withhold one's admiration.

Such are the masters who have furnished me with the rules I have set forth in my book, which has been examined by the master who, since Lully's death, has composed the ballets of the Opéra, and under whose guidance have been trained the most skilful dancers of the day. My labour having been approved by so high an authority, I cannot but pride myself on having attained some measure of success.

CONTENTS

PART I

		PAGE
I.	Of the Manner of Holding the Body	1
II.	Of the Manner of Walking Well	2
III.	Of the Positions and their Origin	5
IV.	Of the First Position	5
V.	Of the Second Position	6
VI.	Of the Third Position	9
VII.	Of the Fourth Position	9
VIII.	Of the Fifth Position	13
IX.	Of Honours in General	13
X.	Of the Manner of Taking off One's Hat and Putting it on Again	15
XI.	Of Honours of Different Kinds	20
XII.	Of Honours Backwards	27
XIII.	Of the Manner in which Ladies should Walk and Comport Themselves	30
XIV.	Of the Different Kinds of Honours	31
XV.	Of the Honours to be Made on Entering a Room or an Assembly	36
XVI.	Of the Ceremonial Observed at the King's Grand Ball	37
XVII.	Of the Manner of Behaving Genteely at Formal Balls	39

		PAGE
XVIII.	OF THE MANNER OF MAKING THE HONOURS BEFORE DANCING	41
XIX.	A DISCOURSE ON MOVEMENTS IN GENERAL	45
XX.	OF THE MANNER OF EXECUTING DEMI-COUPÉS	47
XXI.	OF THE PAS DE MENUET AND THE EASIEST MANNER OF PERFORMING IT TO DIFFERENT SIDES	52
XXII.	OF THE MENUET AND THE MANNER OF DANCING IT CORRECTLY	55
XXIII.	OF THE GRACES THAT MAY BE INTRODUCED INTO THE MENUET AND THE CARE THAT SHOULD BE TAKEN TO DANCE IT UNIFORMLY	63
XXIV.	OF THE CARRIAGE OF THE ARMS IN THE MENUET	66
XXV.	OF THE CONTRETEMPS OF THE MENUET AND THE MANNER OF PERFORMING IT	71
XXVI.	OF THE COURANTE IN GENERAL	74
XXVII.	OF THE TEMPS DE COURANTE, OR PAS GRAVE	76
XXVIII.	OF THE PAS DE BOURRÉE AND FLEURET	78
XXIX.	OF COUPÉS OF DIFFERENT KINDS	82
XXX.	OF COUPÉS OF MOVEMENT	84
XXXI.	OF THE PAS TOMBÉ AND PAS DE GAILLARDE	86
XXXII.	OF PIROUETTES	88
XXXIII.	OF THE BALANCÉ	90
XXXIV.	OF THE PAS DE SISSONNE	91

CONTENTS

		PAGE
XXXV. OF THE PAS DE RIGAUDON	. .	93
XXXVI. OF JETÉS, OR DEMI-CABRIOLES	. .	94
XXXVII. OF THE CONTRETEMPS OF THE GAVOTTE, OR CONTRETEMPS EN AVANT	. .	95
XXXVIII. OF THE DIFFERENT KINDS OF CONTRETEMPS DE CÔTÉ	. . . . .	96
XXXIX. OF CHASSÉS OF DIFFERENT KINDS	.	100
XL. OF SAILLIES OR PAS ECHAPPÉS	. .	105
XLI. OF THE OUVERTURE DE JAMBE	. .	106
XLII. OF BATTEMENTS OF DIFFERENT KINDS	.	110

PART II

I. A DISCOURSE ON THE ARMS AND OF THE IMPORTANCE OF KNOWING HOW TO MOVE THEM GRACEFULLY	. . .	113
II. OF THE POSITION OF THE ARMS AND THEIR CORRECT ELEVATION	. .	114
III. OF THE DIFFERENT MOVEMENTS OF THE ARMS	. . . . . .	116
IV. OF THE MANNER OF MOVING THE WRIST		117
V. OF THE MOVEMENT OF THE ELBOW AND SHOULDER	. . . . .	119
VI. OF THE OPPOSITION OF THE ARMS TO THE FEET	. . . . . .	121
VII. OF THE MANNER OF MOVING THE ARMS IN THE TEMPS DE COURANTE AND DEMI-COUPÉS EN ARRIÈRE	. .	124

Contents

		PAGE
VIII.	Of the Manner of Moving the Arms with Pas de Bourrée or Fleurets	130
IX.	Of the Manner of Moving the Arms with Different Kinds of Coupés	133
X.	Of the Manner of Moving the Arms in Coupés of Movement	135
XI.	Of the Manner of Moving the Arms in the Pas Tombé and Pas de Gaillarde	136
XII.	Of the Manner of Moving the Arms in Pirouettes	137
XIII.	Of the Manner of Moving the Arms with Balancés	140
XIV.	Of the Manner of Moving the Arms in the Pas de Sissonne	140
XV.	Of the Manner of Moving the Arms in Pas de Rigaudon and Jetés	142
XVI.	Of the Manner of Moving the Arms in Contretemps of the Gavotte	143
XVII.	Of the Manner of Moving the Arms with the Contretemps ouvert or Contretemps de Chaconne	146
XVIII.	Of the Manner of Moving the Arms with the Contretemps Ballonné	148
XIX.	Of the Different Manners of Moving the Arms with all Kinds of Chassés	149
XX.	Of the Manner of Moving the Arms in Saillies or Pas Echappés	150

THE DANCING MASTER

Part One

CHAPTER I

Of the Manner of Holding the Body

TO teach well it is essential that the master should begin fitly. But the pupil's high spirits, or, more often, the burden of his studies, tend to make him forgetful of the greater part of his exercises, particularly those relating to dancing. These are by no means rated at their true value, since it is through them that we acquire that grace and distinguished manner for which our nation is famed. Hence, I have prepared a method of instruction by means of which the master may train his pupil in one step after another, at the same time teaching him the different movements of the arms which are appropriate to the various steps in dancing. But, as it is essential that the pupil should know how to comport himself in a graceful manner, this is explained in this first chapter and represented in Fig. 1, which faces page 2.

The head must be held erect without any suggestion of stiffness, the shoulders pressed well back, for this expands the chest and affords more grace to the body. The arms should hang at the sides, the hands be neither quite open nor quite closed, the waist steady, the legs straight and the feet turned outwards. I have endeavoured to make this figure as expressive as possible, so that after consulting it there should be no difficulty in placing the body in the correct position.

I have selected for my figure the pose of a person about to walk; the left foot is placed in front, with the right foot ready to take a step forwards or sideways, for since the body is supported on the left foot the right may move with ease. I hope that in guarding against defects no one will be so stupid as to appear stiff or awkward, which faults are as bad as affectation; good breeding demands that pleasing and easy manner which can only be gained by dancing.

CHAPTER II

Of the Manner of Walking Well

THE body being placed as shown is ready to perform whatever may be required, for this is the position taken whether you wish to walk, bow, or dance. A knowledge of how to walk correctly is very useful, because on this depends the first requisite for dancing, that is, a good deportment. For this reason I beg the reader to pay attention to the easy method I am about to describe, which consists entirely of natural movements.

Suppose that you have the left foot in front, as already shown, and the weight of the body is placed on it, then simultaneously the right knee bends and the heel rises, owing to the weight being placed on the left foot, which consequently causes the right to rise. This is effected by the knee which, being bent, endeavours to straighten, which it does by passing in front of the body. Take care, however, that the foot be not passed forwards beyond the distance of a foot, which is the correct length of a step. The heel must be placed on the ground before the toe, which throws the body forwards on the foot put down; whereas, if the toe be the first to be placed on the ground,

Fig. 1. *The Position of the Body*

the body will be thrown backwards, which will be found very tiring.

The legs must be well extended in their turn, the hips well turned outwards, because the legs turn on them. This is incontestable, since this joint controls and directs the knees and the feet. When I have just said that the legs must be well extended in turn, whichever one you move, keep the knees straight, which will prevent your crossing your steps. This defect is common to many persons through carelessness; again, keep the knees outwards and the legs extended; this prevents their becoming knock-kneed, and even aids the knee-cap to return to a better position.

I have also said that the legs must be extended when they are moved forwards; this is to prevent their being too open or too close together. I am certain that if due care be exercised the faults I have indicated will be avoided. The rate of walking should be moderate, neither too quick nor too slow. One suggests heedlessness, the other indolence; avoid these two extremes.

I have stated that the head must be erect and the waist steady, for by these means the body is maintained in a suitable position, and will not roll. As for the position of the arms, they must remain extended by the side of the body, taking care that if a step be made with the right foot, the left arm makes a little forward movement which balances it, and even comes quite naturally. But, as many ignore this action through carelessness, I am obliged to make this very important observation.

A step being to pass the foot forwards, backwards, or sideways, applies equally to either foot when walking; but, as regards dancing, the term *pas* implies a combination of several steps which sometimes differ in many movements, but which together make up only one step, as, for example, in the *pas de menuet, pas de courante, pas de bourrée*, and many others which I shall teach you how to perform. But as all these movements must be considered in turn, and as the rules which govern them are founded on the five positions, these will be explained in the following chapters.

CHAPTER III

Of the Positions and their Origin

WHAT is termed a position is nothing more than a separation or bringing together of the feet according to a fixed distance, while the body is maintained upright and in equilibrium without any appearance of constraint, whether one walks, dances, or comes to a stop. These positions were discovered through the application of the late Monsieur Beauchamps,[1] who wished to give a definite foundation to the art.

Before his time these positions were unknown, which proves his deep knowledge of this art. They must be regarded as indispensable and unbreakable rules. I learned from him that, according to the rules of his age, there were five kinds of *pas*,[2] and from them were derived the other *pas* used in dancing. As he had a considerable aptitude for design, which is as important as music to a composer of ballets, this rare genius found that nothing was more important to maintain the body in a graceful attitude and the steps in a fixed space than to introduce these five positions. Hence, they are to be regarded as indispensable rules which must be kept.

[1] Beauchamps (often written Beauchamp) was the Director of the *Académie Royale de Danse*, Composer and Superintendent of the King's Ballets in 1661; and *Maître de Ballet* of the *Académie Royale de Musique* in 1671. He continued in this post until 1687. Died in 1695.

[2] *Cf.* Feuillet (R.A.) *Chorégraphie, ou l'Art de De'crire la Danse.* 1701. p. 9 : " *Quoy que la quantité des Pas dont on se sert dans la Danse soit presqu'innombrable, on les reduit neanmoins à cinq* . . . . *qu'on appelle pas droit, pas ouvert, pas rond, pas tortillé & pas battu.*"

CHAPTER IV

Of the First Position

THESE positions, as I have just remarked, are only to give a correct proportion to the steps, so that the body is maintained in a perpendicular line. I do not say equilibrium; that is a different matter, which I shall explain later.

I give the explanation and representation of each position in turn, as well as its use. But, to understand them the more easily, it must be stated that this figure, like the others, differs only in the positions of the legs and feet; the body must always be upright and supported on both feet.

In the first position (see Fig. 2) the legs are straight, the two heels one against the other, and the feet turned out equally. Its use is in closed steps and in bending movements, because all steps which begin with *demi-coupés* should be taken from this position. The reason is that if you bent, and one foot were behind the other, the knees would have a tendency to turn inwards; whereas, if the heels be close together, the knees turn outwards equally. Again, the body appears more erect, which I shall explain at length in the manner of making the movements, since here I only intend to explain and demonstrate the positions.

CHAPTER V

Of the Second Position

THIS second position (see Fig. 3) shows the distance to be observed in open steps, which are made sideways; it is represented by both legs placed wide apart, but there should not be more than the space of a foot between them, which is the correct proportion of the step and the true position of the body supported on both legs, which is shown by the shoulders being at the same height. That is the reason why the body can easily be supported on either leg without any forced movement; it is used in open steps which, like the fifth position, are employed for travelling sideways, the fifth being used for crossed steps.

It must be noted that both feet are on the same line, the legs straight and the feet turned equally outwards, so that the weight of the body rests on both legs, as in the first position.

I beg the reader to learn these positions by heart, not only

Fig. 2. The First Position

Fig. 3. The Second Position

for the correct proportion of the steps, but also for the manner of making them, because, later on, when I give the position from which a step commences and that in which it finishes, he will be obliged to return to the beginning of the book, which will hinder the execution of the step.

CHAPTER VI

Of the Third Position

THIS position (see Fig. 4) is for enclosed and other steps; it is called *emboîture*, and not unreasonably, for this position is only perfect when the legs are well extended and near each other. It is done with the legs and feet close together, so that no light can be seen between them, and they join like the sides of a box. Therefore, I have drawn this figure carefully to make it the more easily comprehensible, that the eye, which is the mirror of the soul, shall give more force to my powers of expression by affording the reader that clear explanation which I desire to give him.

The body is placed erect on both feet, the left in front but crossed before the heel of the right at the ankle, as shown in the figure. This position is one most necessary to good dancing; it teaches the dancer to stand firm, to straighten the knees, and constrains him to that regularity which is the beauty of this art.

CHAPTER VII

Of the Fourth Position

THIS position (see Fig. 5), serves to regulate the steps forwards or backwards, and gives them that correct distance which should be observed whether in walking or dancing.

Fig. 4. The Third Position

Fig. 5. The Fourth Position

The body is placed as in the other positions, with the exception of the feet, in which the left is in front and the right behind. But, while it is not so easy to observe from this viewpoint the distance which should lie between the legs, as it would be were they seen in profile, yet an examination of the perspective shows that the left foot is more advanced than the right. Moreover, I decided to choose this view because all the parts are in sight. Observe that in this position the feet are placed one in front of the other, and are in a straight line without being crossed, especially when dancing. For if the feet were crossed when making a forward movement it would be impossible to rise with the same ease; furthermore, the body would be thrown out of equilibrium and be contorted.

In walking, if the feet be crossed, the person moves obliquely and the body is thrown awry, which must be avoided with the greatest care. It is true that this depends on the master's vigilance, for, sometimes, at the beginning, bad faults are contracted which eventually require all the trouble in the world to correct, and, however good the master may be, if the pupil himself do not work hard to correct them he cannot succeed.

But I shall be told that a person has no bent for dancing; to which I reply we can always learn when we wish to do so. This is not difficult to prove. Do we not walk? Do we not make bows? Thus, it is simply a question of devoting ourselves to making them well, and walking elegantly; and when you are able to make a graceful bow you unconsciously acquire a taste for dancing.

I shall then be told that one ought to possess a considerable aptitude to dance well. I agree; but goodwill will carry forward the least gifted, and I shall add further that such persons can dance passably well without any aptitude whatever, for dancing is no more than knowing how to bend and straighten the knees at the proper time.

CHAPTER VIII

Of the Fifth Position

THIS last position (see Fig. 6) is, as I have already said, for crossed steps and for moving sideways, whether to the right or left. It is inseparable from the second. From these two positions the dancer can move to any side without turning, and with the body facing. But, to perform it well, the heel of the foot that crosses must not pass beyond the toe of the rear foot; this would be against all rules, for the body would be thrown out of balance. Moreover, if the foremost foot were crossed farther than the toe of the rear foot, the latter would be forced inwards. This can be observed in the figure, where the foot is crossed only so far as the rule permits.

In all these positions I have shown the body supported equally on both legs, which, by the distance observed, proves that one foot may be raised, while the body rests on the other, without any strained movement. I shall not speak of the false positions, because they seem to me useless for young persons to learn, but leave their explanation to the discretion of those masters who care to teach them to their pupils. However, they are rarely encountered, save in turning steps, or in *pas de ballet*.

CHAPTER IX

Of Honours in General

A VERY necessary matter for everyone, whatever their station, to be informed upon, is the correct manner of raising one's hat and making a graceful bow; but in general it is that which receives the least care, whereas everything shows that both should be well done. In the first place, this excites admiration in others for us, and brings further advantages in its train. It inclines a person to show us consideration by regarding us as persons who

Fig. 6. The Fifth Position

have known how to profit from the education we have received. But as bows are made in different ways, according to the particular occasions for which they are required, I shall explain each one separately, according to the figure representing the principal movements to be made by the body, after I have shown in the following chapter the manner of taking off the hat and putting it on again—a very useful accomplishment, above all for young persons, whom it is difficult to convince of the importance thereof.

CHAPTER X

Of the Manner of Taking off One's Hat and Putting it on Again

HAVING explained the positions and spoken of bowing in a general way, and since a bow is not made without first raising one's hat, I shall, in order to follow the plan I have in mind, make it the subject of the present chapter. This treats of the manner of raising and replacing the hat; also how to avoid those faults in one or the other, which may arise through carelessness.

The body being placed according to the aforesaid rules, if you desire to salute someone, the arm must be raised to the height of the shoulder (as shown in Fig. 7), first, having the hand open (2), secondly, bending the elbow to take hold of the hat. This causes the hand to describe a semicircle, according to the words: *The bend of the elbow*, the centre of the circle being the elbow itself.

The elbow being bent, as shown in Fig. 8, and the hand open, as in Fig. 7, it must be carried to the head, which should remain still; then place the thumb against the forehead with the four fingers resting on the brim. On closing the hand the pressure of the thumb will cause the hat to rise, while the four fingers will grasp it. Then, raising the arm a little more, lift the hat above the head, extend the arm in a line with the shoulder (and at right angles to the body) and lower it to the side. This movement is termed: *The fall of the arm*, and is shown in Fig. 8.

Fig. 7. The First Movement to take off the Hat

Fig. 8. The Second Movement to take off the Hat

Fig. 9 represents the manner of holding the hat at the side, crown behind.

All the different attitudes represented by these three figures are only to show the different ſtages in the complete movement, for they are not intended to mean that there should be an interval between each part of the whole movement, which would be absurd. What I mean is that there should be no pause, and that the three actions should be continuous, so that they appear to be but one single movement; because it is merely one movement divided into three—which seemed to me the beſt method of explaining each action; that is, to raise the arm from the side, bending the elbow; to carry it to the head and take hold of the hat; to raise it and allow the arm to fall to the side again.

To put the hat on again the same order is to be observed; that is, raise the arm from the side to the height of the shoulder and, bending the elbow, put the hat on the head, pressing it down firmly by the brim once only. But do not press the hand on the top of the crown, which would be a breach of good manners; for the head should not attempt to assiſt the operation; the hand and arm should put the hat on. On the other hand, the hat muſt not be forced down too ſtrongly, since then it would be difficult to remove again; the hat is only to cover and grace the head. Care muſt also be taken never to hold the hat by the crown, nor to carry the arm and hand too far forwards, for that would cause the face to be hidden; nor to drop the head and allow the hat to fall over the face carelessly, which would look very ill.

In my opinion the moſt graceful manner of wearing a hat is to place it over the forehead a little above the eyebrows, pressing the hand lightly on the brim, so that the hat is placed almoſt level, but the peak should be a few degrees lower than the back. The button should be on the left side, and the peak or point over the left eye, which uncovers the face. For to wear the hat tilted backwards gives one a foolish and idiotic appearance, juſt as to wear it pressed down too much in front gives one a cunning, angry, or dreamy look; whereas, if the hat be worn as I have directed, you will appear well bred, modeſt, and agreeable.

Fig. 9. The Manner of holding the Hat by the Side

CHAPTER XI

Of Honours of Different Kinds

HAVING in the previous chapter informed the reader how to take off his hat, I shall now speak of each bow in turn, to enable him to recognise the difference between them, by showing him how to perform them properly, according to the various occasions that from time to time may arise.

I will begin with the bow forwards. Keep the body upright and slide forwards the foot that is in front (for the purpose of my drawing I have assumed this to be the left) until it is in the fourth position, as shown in Figs. 10 and 11. These show the uprightness of the body when one foot is advanced, for it must be understood that the body is not to bend or incline until the foot has been moved, because the body follows the legs, and what it should do afterwards is explained in the other two plates in which the body is shown bent (see Figs. 12 and 13).

I say then that you should move the foot gently forwards, leaving the weight of the body on the rear foot, the knee of which is forced to bend on account of the weight of the body, whereas the front leg should be well extended. But the inclination of the body is greater or less, according to the rank of the person you salute. The head also is inclined, and this is one of the essential parts of the bow. In bending the waist, do not straighten the knee of the rear foot, for that would cause the hip to rise and twist the body sideways, instead of your assuming the position I have shown, where all parts are balanced in opposition. When you rise, do so with the same ease with which you bowed, and, in rising, transfer the weight of the body to the front foot. This permits the rear one to be ready to move forwards or sideways to perform another bow, which is usually made backwards, and which I shall explain when dealing with the honours to be made on entering a room.

In regard to the passing bow, this is done in the same manner as the bow forwards, save that the body must be

Fig. 10. *The First Posture of a Bow Forwards*

Fig. 11. *The First Posture of a Bow Forwards*
(View in profile)

Fig. 12. The Second Posture of a Bow Forwards

*Fig. 13. The Second Posture of a Bow Forwards
(View in profile)*

turned diagonally towards the persons you salute. That is, you turn half-sideways towards them, sliding forwards the foot that is nearest them, whether it be the right or the left, bending the waist and inclining the head at the same time, as shown in Fig. 14.

If the salute be made to the left side, then it is the left foot which slides forwards, and similarly in the case of the right side; but, as this bow is used in different places, it is important that I should cite the conditions under which it must be performed with the utmost nicety. For example, when you are walking in the streets, the bow need only be a very slight one; it is, as it were, a bow made while walking.

But in the case of bows made in fashionable promenades, such as the Tuileries or similar places to which the best society resorts, they must not be made with the same slightness, but performed with ceremony and grace.

Note also that people, when promenading, customarily carry their hats under their arms. If, therefore, a person of superior rank salute you, take your hat in your right hand and afterwards make a deep bow to show your greater respect.

Another important observation is that when you bend your body do not incline the head so low as to hide the face, a fault which is rendered the greater because the person is in doubt as to whether you desire to salute him or not. Hence, before you begin your bow, look modestly at the person; this is termed *directing your bow before you make it*.

I am convinced that if due attention be paid to these observations, every one will make his bows with all that grace they merit. But, as there is no better method of learning than that of constantly repeating what one wishes to retain, I take this opportunity of exhorting those young gentlemen who are studying at academies and colleges to devote themselves to the art of making bows, since in the course of their comings and goings they are continually bound to meet their masters or tutors, and be obliged to pay or return a salute. I counsel them to acquire this art

*Fig. 14. The Posture of a Passing Bow
Saluting on the Left Side*

so that it becomes habitual to them, that they will not feel out of countenance, as frequently happens, should they find themselves placed in unfamiliar company or unusual surroundings.

CHAPTER XII

Of Honours Backwards

THESE bows are performed quite differently from those forwards and are more ceremonious, for this reason they demand more care, but this is set off by the pleasure experienced in being distinguished from the common herd. Suppose then the hat to be held in the hand and the feet placed in the fourth position, as shown in Fig. 15, and the body supported on the left foot so that the right is ready to move sideways to the second position [1]; but, in making this step, the heel should be the first to be placed on the ground which makes it easier for the body to balance. Then the body is inclined according to Fig. 16, which shows the feet in the second position.

The weight of the body is then transferred to the right foot, and the left, being ready to move, you gently draw it behind the right so that it is in the third position, raising the body as the foot is drawn behind, which restores the body to equilibrium and is the extent of your bow.

I have seen many people bend from the waist and draw back the foot simultaneously, which I find very good; but the manner I have described is, in my opinion, still more graceful and has a more distinguished appearance.

I have said that this bow differs from that forwards; this is true for, to perform the bow forwards, the first movement consists in sliding the foot forwards and immediately inclining so that there is no interval between the two actions; whereas, in the bow backwards, the body and head is inclined before the foot is moved,[2] but the interval

[1] The right foot must be carried forward also to obtain a true second position.
[2] *I.e.*, closed in the third position.

Fig. 15. *The First Posture of a Bow Backwards*

Fig. 16. The Second Posture of a Bow Backwards

between these movements should be short, so that they appear almost simultaneous, and also to avoid any suggestion of affectation.

The best way to acquire facility in making these bows is to perform several in succession, which is easier since, the foot being drawn backwards in completion of the step and the weight of the body transferred to it, the front foot is moved sideways ready to begin another and so continues to perform several. But when you find it easy to make the movements with one foot, they should be practised with the other, so that you feel equally at ease whichever foot be used.

CHAPTER XIII

Of the Manner in which Ladies should Walk and Comport Themselves

I HAVE no doubt but that I should be accused of indifference or of knowing only how to teach men, did I lack enthusiasm and care for the instruction of the fair sex, who are the soul of dancing and accord it all the brilliance it possesses, did I omit the most graceful beings fashioned by Nature. For, without ladies, dancing would not be so animated, because their presence evokes that ardent and noble emulation which we put forth when we dance together, particularly in the case of those who dance well, of whom there is a goodly number.

In my opinion nothing is more pleasing in a company than to see two persons of the opposite sex dance together correctly. What applause they evoke from every one!

For this reason, apart from what I have already said in the preceding chapters concerning the manner of walking, which applies equally to either sex, the same remarks are necessary for ladies, because they must turn out their feet and straighten their knees, although some persons assert that it is impossible to perceive faults in these actions. To correct this fallacy, above all in the case of young people who are inclined to be careless, let them draw their own conclusions by standing in front of a mirror and taking several steps according to the manner I have described in the previous chapters. Then let them walk carelessly and they will find that they have a quite different appearance, and must admit that by holding the head erect, the body upright and the knees straight, their steps are made with more assurance.

Lastly, I have made what seems to me a very just observation regarding the manner of holding the head. A lady, however graceful her deportment, will be judged in a quite different way from a man. For example, if she hold her head erect and her body upright, without affectation or boldness, it will be said: "There goes a fine lady." If she carry herself carelessly, she will be regarded as indifferent; if she hold herself too far forward, she will be termed indolent; finally, if she stoop, she will be looked upon as dreamy or shy; and there are many other examples which I shall not cite here, lest I be accused of prolixity.

I only hope that young ladies will pay attention to the easy method I have described, so as never to fall into the faults I have mentioned and on which account I have placed this figure (Fig. 17), which demonstrates their correct deportment when walking. A lady should carry the head erect, the shoulders low, and the arms bent and held backwards close to the body, while the hands should be in front, one over the other, clasping a fan. But remember, above all, no affectation.

CHAPTER XIV

Of the Different Kinds of Honours

LADIES do not labour under the same difficulties as men in making their honours; it suffices for them to have a good deportment, to turn their feet well outwards, slide them properly, bend the knees equally, hold the head

Fig. 17. The Deportment of a Lady when Walking

and body erect, and the arms well disposed, as shown in Fig. 18, which illustrates the essentials to be observed.

Their honours may be of three kinds as for ourselves. That is: the courtesy forwards, the passing courtesy, and the courtesy backwards. The most respectful is the last which contains a short pause; moreover, the degree of bending is greater.

I shall begin with the courtesy forwards. Slide the front foot to the fourth position and leave the weight of the body supported equally on both legs, then gently bend the knees without inclining from the waist, which must be held upright without that shaking which often arises when the feet are badly placed. Hence they must not be too close together nor too far apart. When you have bent the knees sufficiently, rise with the same smoothness; this makes the conclusion of the bow.

The passing courtesy is performed similarly except that when you meet a person you take two or three steps forwards before beginning your courtesy. Look at the persons you wish to salute, simultaneously directing your courtesy and turning half-sideways towards them. Then slide forwards the foot nearest to them and sink and rise very gently, taking care to transfer the weight of the body to the front foot in order to be ready to move the rear one.

Fig. 19 is intended to represent the correct manner of performing this courtesy. The lady salutes to the left side, the head is turned similarly; the left shoulder is drawn backwards as shown. But since these courtesies are used in promenades and other places of ceremony, it should be noted that, when you salute a person of superior quality, the courtesy backwards, which is more respectful, and not the passing courtesy, should be employed.

This courtesy backwards is made by carrying either foot to the side so that it falls into the second position, the weight of the body resting on the foot that was moved, while the other is drawn to it so that the heels meet and the feet are in the first position. Then bend the knees equally and very low, and rise with the same care with which you sank. But should you wish to make a second courtesy,

Fig. 18. A Courtesy Forwards

Fig. 19. A Passing Courtesy

leave the weight of the body on the foot you have drawn up, carry the other foot to the side and close in the first position as before. For this reason I have drawn this Fig. 18 which represents a courtesy direct or facing the person saluted. I find this very necessary for you to come to a correct understanding. Care must also be taken not to draw the foot and bend the knees at the same time, as this destroys the balance and produces shakiness.

I have already said that the two heels should be close to each other, because when you bend the knees in such a position, turning them outwards, neither is advanced before the other; whereas, by drawing one foot behind the other, one knee is brought forwards and inclined to turn inwards, two faults which must be avoided.

CHAPTER XV

Of the Honours to be Made on Entering a Room or an Assembly

WHEN you enter a room, take off your hat with the right hand as explained in Chapter X., and take two or three steps forwards so that the door will not be in your way, and also to give yourself time to direct your bows. Then make your first bow forwards, but, on rising, transfer the weight of the body to the foot moved forwards, and carry the rear one to the side so that it is in the second position, ready to make your bow backwards.

Having made these two bows, you enter. If there be much company to your right and left, make your passing bows as you go among the assembled persons. But should you wish to converse with some one, you make the same bows as on entering, and in leaving him you make two bows backwards, and such other passing bows as politeness demands, which has no limits. In this respect, be guided by the precepts of the best society.

Having taught the manner of entering a room, there

remains, in continuing the instruction necessary for a noble youth, to afford an idea of a Ball and the manner of comporting yourself with politeness so that you will be asked to dance, or be able to invite a person to dance with you, which matters shall be explained in the next chapter.

CHAPTER XVI

Of the Ceremonial observed at the King's Grand Ball

I BELIEVED it impossible to give a description more likely to inspire regard for the ceremonies and rules of private Balls than first to attempt some brief account of the King's Grand Ball, since it is the most important of all such functions and should serve as a model for private Balls in regard to the order of the proceedings, and the respect and politeness to be observed thereat.

In the first place, none is admitted to the royal circle save Princes and Princesses of the Blood Royal, then Dukes and Peers, and Duchesses, and afterwards the other Lords and Ladies of the Court according to their rank. The Ladies are seated in front, while the Lords are placed behind them. Nevertheless, I have ventured to represent the latter standing, to avoid confusion in my figures, and to make them more easily seen (Fig. 20).

Every one being thus placed in order, when His Majesty wishes the Ball to begin he rises, and the whole company does likewise.

The King takes up his position at that end of the room where the dancing is to begin, which is near the musicians. In the time of the late King,[1] the Queen danced with him, or, in her absence, the first Princess of the Blood, and placed themselves first. Then the company took up their station behind them, two by two, according to their rank. That is to say: *Monseigneur*[2] and *Madame la Dauphine*,[3] *Monsieur*[4]

[1] Louis XIV.
[2] The King's eldest son.
[3] The title of the wife of the King's eldest son.
[4] The title of the King's brother.

and *Madame*,[1] then the other Princes and Lords. The Lords stood on the left side, the Ladies on the right. Retaining this order, they made their bows in turn. Afterwards the King and Queen led the *Branle* with which all Court Balls opened, and all the Lords and Ladies followed Their Majesties, each on their own side. At the conclusion of the strain, the King and Queen went to the end of the line, then the next couple led the *Branle* in their turn, after which they took up their position behind Their Majesties. This continued until all the couples had danced and the King and Queen were at the head again.

Then they danced the *Gavotte* in the same order as the *Branle*, each couple successively retiring to the end of the line. The dance finished, they made the same bows on parting as those with which the Ball opened.

Then came the *danses à deux*. Formerly the *Courante* was danced after the *Branles*, and Louis XIV. of happy memory danced it better than any member of his Court, as I shall show later. But nowadays the *Menuet* is danced after the *Branles*.

Therefore, when the King has danced the first *Menuet*, he goes to his seat and every one sits down, for while His Majesty is dancing all stand. Then the Prince who is to dance next after His Majesty is seated, makes him a very profound bow, and then goes to the Queen or the first Princess of the Blood, and together they make the same bows as before the dance. Afterwards they dance the *Menuet*, and at the conclusion make the same bows again. Then the Lord makes a very low bow to the Princess on leaving her, because she will not appear again before the King.

At the same time, he advances three or four steps forwards, to salute with another bow the Princess or Lady whose turn is next, to invite her to dance with him. Then he awaits her so that together they may make a low bow to the King, as shown by these two numbers, 1, 2, when they descend a little lower, according to the numbers 3, 4, and make the customary bows before dancing, and perform

[1] The wife of the King's brother.

Fig. 20. The King's Grand Ball

the *Menuet*. At the end of this dance they make the usual bows. Finally, on leaving her, he makes a bow backwards and returns to his place, when the Lady observes the same ceremonial to invite another Prince, and so on to the end.

But if His Majesty desire another dance to be performed, one of the First Gentlemen of the Bed Chamber announces his wish, which does not prevent the same bows being observed.

CHAPTER XVII

Of the Manner of Behaving Genteely at Formal Balls

AS I proposed in this treatise to teach the noble youth how to behave in places where fashion calls them, and since Balls permit a certain freedom owing to the ease with which all classes of persons may gain admittance, including a number boasting I know not what birth and rank, who, lacking in good breeding, have no scruples in upsetting the correct order of procedure, I shall therefore deal here with the ceremonies that must be observed, so that my readers may be prepossessed in their favour by their politeness.

Since at all regulated Balls a King and Queen are chosen, it is they who according to rule begin the dancing, and when the first *Menuet* is concluded, the Queen invites another gentleman to come and dance with her, and after they have danced he takes the Queen back to her place and politely asks her whom she wishes him to take out, and, after he has bowed to her, he makes another bow to the person whom he must take out, to invite her to dance with him.

But if the person invited be speaking to some one and cannot come immediately, he must return to that side of the room from which the dance is begun and await her. He must be attentive when this lady comes to him and pay her that respect which polite society requires to be observed.

When you have finished your *Menuet* or other dance, make the same bows at the conclusion as you performed at the beginning, but, apart from that, the gentleman makes another one backwards and takes up his former position to give place to those whose turn it is to dance next.

But if you are asked to dance again, you must, when it is your turn to invite a lady, choose the one who asked you in the first place, otherwise you would commit a grave breach of good manners. This rule applies equally to ladies.

Hence, when you are invited to dance, you must go to that part of the room where the dancing begins and make the customary bows before dancing. But if the lady you have chosen excuses herself on the ground that she rarely dances, or has been learning but a short while, you will, having concluded your bows, lead her back to her place. Then you will choose another lady, and having made your bow to her, invite her to dance with you in order not to disturb the order of the Ball.

But should you be pressed to dance and have already refused once before, you must not dance for all that Ball, whatever the reasons urged, for this would slight the person that invited you first. This rule should be observed by members of both sexes.

Those who are responsible for the procedure at the Ball should take care that every one dances in his turn, to avoid confusion and discontent. As regards those who come masked, these should be made to dance first, that they may invite those of their company afterwards. Particular respect should be paid to persons in masks, for these often conceal people of the highest rank.

I do not doubt but that when all these precautions are taken, both those who officiate at Balls and those who form the company, will be distinguished by their good manners and breeding.

As regards family dances, at which the company generally consists of parents and their friends and relations, the same ceremonial should be observed as at Balls. That is, each member of the company should know how to invite a person to dance, to make his bow properly and to be ready, when he has been invited to dance, to return the compliment with the same politeness with which he has been asked. Above all, I pray young persons for whom such dances are often arranged to pay heed to the rules that their masters should have taught them, that they may reflect credit on the instruction they have received.

CHAPTER XVIII

Of the Manner of Making the Honours before Dancing

ALTHOUGH the bows made before dancing are performed similarly to those backwards, they nevertheless require some particular instructions. Hence I beg you to pay attention to the rules set forth, so that they may be well done, which is of importance. Since, in whatever company you are, generally every one is curious to see who is going to dance, and if you display a pleasing grace you will make so favourable an impression that, should your dancing fall short of perfection, it will be said that you know how to make a graceful bow.

I must warn you that you should have your gloves on before you take up your position to dance, for it would be most ill-mannered to keep your partner waiting.

I assume then that you are standing side by side, the right foot in front in the fourth position, as shown in Fig. 21. I shall not again describe the manner of taking off the hat, having already dealt with this matter. But I shall only say that it must be taken off with the left hand, following the same rules as those previously laid down for the right.

The body being supported on the left foot (1), the right foot in front (2), take off the hat with the left hand and allow it to fall to the side like the right (3), and at the same time offer your right hand to the lady (4), looking at her.

Fig. 22 depicts the lady and gentleman in their proper places; the lady on the right, the gentleman on the left.

Fig. 21. The Gentleman presenting his Hand to Dance

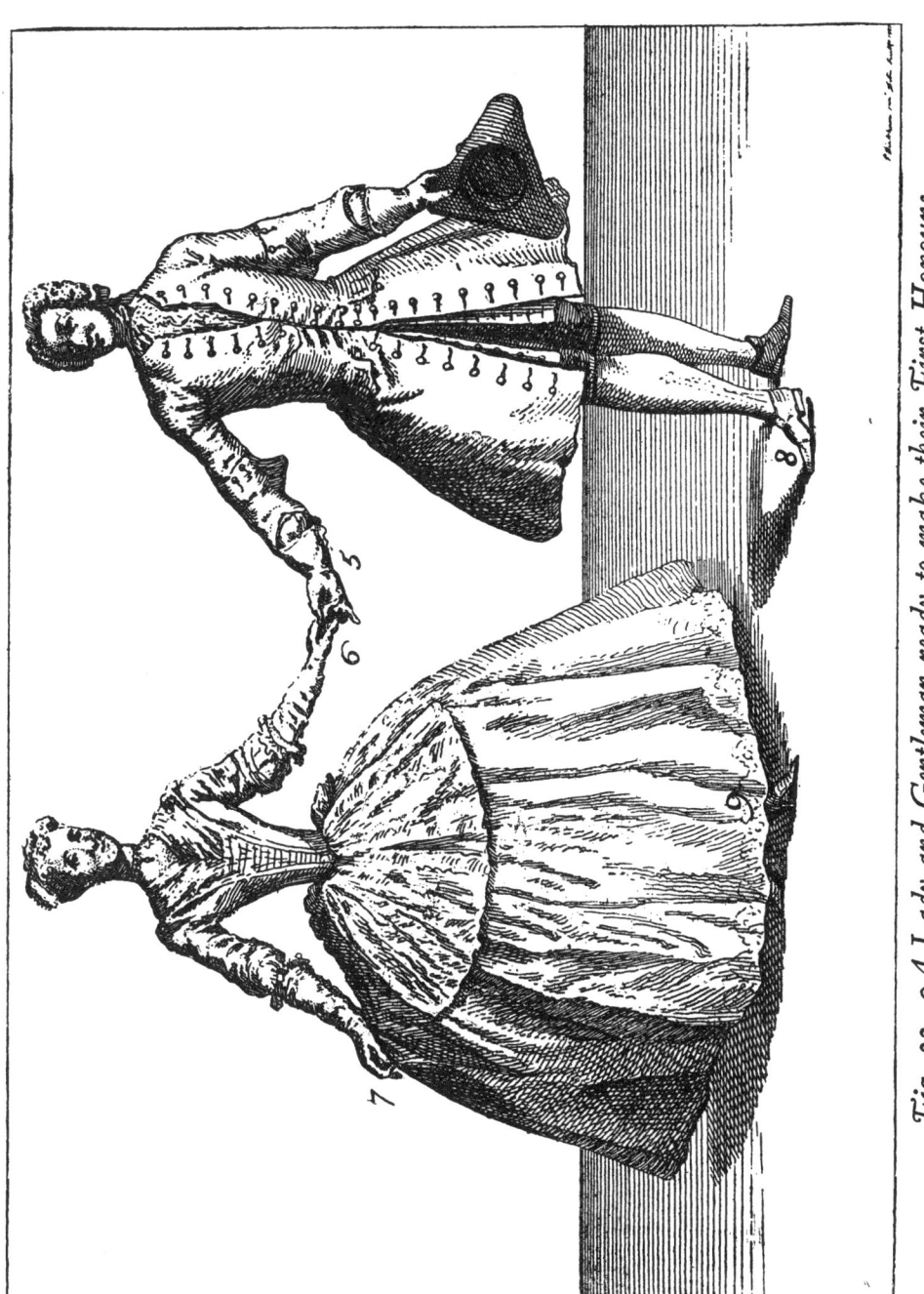

Fig. 22. *A Lady and Gentleman ready to make their First Honours*

standing side by side on the same line. The gentleman holds the lady by the hand, so that his is below (5), and hers above (6). Her right arm is kept at the side with the thumb holding her skirt (7), because if the arm were turned outwards, the hand would be concealed by the folds.

From this attitude the man moves his right foot sideways to the right (8), which is the second position, while the lady moves her left foot sideways to the left (9), in the same position.

The man, having moved his foot to the second position, transfers the weight of the body to it, and inclines at the same time to make his bow, which is made like the bows backwards, as previously remarked; but, in making this bow, he does not leave hold of the lady's hand, and so that you will understand all the movements, I will set them down in detail.

The body being entirely supported on the right foot, the left is ready to move, but, on beginning to rise from your bow, the left, with the heel raised, slides simultaneously behind the right, a little farther than the third position, which restores the body to its proper equilibrium.

But, on rising, the weight of the body rests on the left foot and you leave hold of the lady's hand, sliding the right foot forwards so that it is crossed a little farther than the fifth position. But in making this step, the body moves differently from other steps, because it turns to the left side while simultaneously the right arm and foot move in the same direction. When you slide the right foot, the left knee bends, causing the weight of the body to be transferred to the right foot, and, by making a half turn to the right, brings you facing the lady.

Then move the left foot sideways to the second position, looking at the lady to direct your bow, bend the waist and incline the head as in the first bow, and, rising, draw the right foot behind. But if you are to dance the *Menuet*, in rising, leave the weight of the body on the left foot, ready to begin your *pas de menuet*[1] with the right. If, however, you are to perform a different dance, you must, after drawing

[1] Minuet step.

the right foot behind, leave the weight on it so as to slide the left forwards simultaneously, which brings you back to whence you made your first bow. Then make a half[1] turn to the left and execute another step with the right foot, returning to the right side, which brings you back facing the company. Then await the beginning of the music before you dance.

As to the lady, she, having the left foot in front in the fourth position, moves it to the second position, and immediately draws the right to it in the first position, then bends both knees equally, as already explained. The first courtesy made, she must leave the weight of the body on the right foot, and slide the left in front, a little farther than the fifth position, to make a half turn to the left, at the same time moving the right foot sideways, which brings her opposite her partner. Then, looking at him, and drawing the left foot close to the right, she bends gently and rises in the same manner, and leaves the weight of the body on the left foot, to be able to begin the *Menuet* with the right.

But if she is to perform a different dance, she must slide the right foot in front, a little farther than the fifth position, and in returning to the place whence she made her first courtesy, make a half[1] turn to the right and move the left foot to the second position, when she will be brought facing the company, to wait until the music bids her begin.

CHAPTER XIX

A Discourse on Movements in General

TO dance well, it is most essential to know how to make the movements, and to perform them well they must be thoroughly understood, and to know them properly one must be acquainted with the laws of motion; which I shall endeavour to teach you according to the rules of the art.

[1] It would seem that a quarter turn is sufficient to return to face the company.

There are three movements from the waist to the feet, that of the hip, knee, and instep; all the different *pas* in dancing are formed from these principal movements.

But they cannot attain perfection until the joints have made their bendings and returned to their original positions, that is to say, until the leg is straight.

I shall begin then by explaining the action of the instep, which can move in two ways; that is, tension and extension, to use the terms of anatomy, which is what we call raising the toe and lowering it.

In my opinion, this action is the most tiring of all, because it supports the whole weight of the body in its equilibrium; nevertheless, this movement is most essential to good dancing. According to the greater or less strength of the instep, so can the leg be extended more or less easily, whether in dancing or jumping. Because when you bend to jump, the instep, by its strength, raises you in a lively manner and enables you to alight *sur la demi-pointe*. The more steps you perform *sur les demi-pointes* the lighter you will appear to dance, but it is the hip which guides the step, while the instep supports the body and perfects the step by enabling it to be executed with lightness.

The movement of the knee is different from this, because it is only perfect when the leg is stretched and the foot pointed, as in *demi-coupés* in which the knee is bent and the toe slightly raised; but when you pass the foot and rise, the instep perfects the movement. Hence the action of the knee is inseparable from that of the instep.

The movement of the hip is quite different; its action is not so apparent, for it is more concealed, nevertheless it controls and orders the other movements, for neither the knee nor the foot could turn did the hips not turn first, which is indisputable, since it is the controlling joint. But there are *pas* in which the hip alone moves, such as *battements terre à terre*, *entrechats* and *cabrioles*, which belong to theatrical dancing. Again, when these *pas* are made in the air, it is the hips only which move the legs, because, to perform such movements properly, the legs must be fully extended. Hence neither the insteps nor the knees move.

But, as I engaged only to give instruction in ballroom dancing, I must not digress by discussing *pas* which demand a far greater executive ability.

CHAPTER XX

Of the Manner of Executing Demi-Coupés

HAVING explained the three movements, I shall describe their manner of employment. As no *pas* in which the knee is bent can be made without flexing that joint, and since in general all *pas* which are composed of several steps begin with a *demi-coupé*, it is immaterial whether it be the right or the left foot, because the movement is the same in both cases. But I shall suppose it to be the right, then the left foot must be in the fourth position front and the weight of the body supported by it as shown in Fig. 23, where the body is placed on the left foot with the right ready to move, having only the toe placed on the ground.

To begin the *demi-coupé*, bring the right foot against the left in the first position and bend both knees equally, keeping the weight of the body on the left foot as shown in Fig. 24, in which both heels are touching but the weight of the body is on the left foot, the right off the ground, both knees equally bent and turned outwards, the waist straight and the head well back.

Keeping the same position, carry the right foot forwards to the fourth position, as shown in Fig. 25, at the same time transferring the weight of the body to it, and rise on the right *demi-pointe* (see Fig. 26 (3)). This may be termed the equilibrium or balance, because the body is supported on one foot only.

But, on rising, the knee must be straightened and the left foot (4), with its knee likewise straightened, brought close to the right heel as shown in Fig. 26. Afterwards the right heel is lowered to the ground, which completes the *pas* and

Fig. 23. The First Posture in the Demi-Coupé

Fig. 24. The Second Posture in the Demi-Coupé

Fig. 25. The Third Posture in the Demi-Coupe

Fig. 26. The Fourth Posture in the Demi-Coupé, showing the Equilibrium or Balance

leaves you in a position ready to make another with the other foot, observing the same rules. Such *pas* can be repeated several times in succession, always taking care to bend the knees well, to rise on the *demi-pointe*, and to straighten the knees with each *demi-coupé*, which *pas* is one of the most useful aids to good dancing, for it enables the knees to be straightened and their strength given to the insteps. Therefore the ability to dance well depends on this first *pas*, since it is only the knowledge of how to bend properly and rise correctly which makes the fine dancer.

This *pas* can be made backwards or sideways in accordance with the same rule, which is that the foot must not be moved forwards until the knees have been bent, which is most important, because pupils very often make their movements incorrectly, and hence are unable to rise with the same ease with which they sank.

CHAPTER XXI

Of the Pas de Menuet and the Easiest Manner of Performing it to Different Sides

HAVING fully explained the easiest manner of making *demi-coupés*, which are the basis and foundation of different *pas*, and since the *Menuet* is the most favoured dance, I shall give you the easiest way to succeed in dancing it well.

First, you must know that the true *pas de menuet* is composed of four steps, which, owing to their being connected, make, however, according to the terminology of the art, but one *pas*. This *pas de menuet* has three movements and a *pas marché sur la demi-pointe* ; that is to say, the first is a *demi-coupé* with the right foot, then one with the left, and a *pas marché sur la demi-pointe* with the right foot, with the knees straight. At the end of this step you quietly lower the right heel to the ground to allow the knee to bend, which causes the left leg to rise and pass forwards, making a *demi-coupé echappé*, which is the third movement of the *pas de menuet* and its fourth step.

The Dancing Master

But since this *pas* is not suited to everyone, because it demands a very strong instep, it is not very much used; and its execution has been simplified by the use of an easier manner consisting of two movements only, which I shall now describe.

You must know that this *pas*, like the other, is composed of four steps. It begins with two *demi-coupés*, the first being made with the right foot, the second with the left, followed by two *pas marchés sur la demi-pointe*, the first with the right foot, the second with the left, executed to two bars of triple time, one called the cadence, the other the counter-cadence. To understand this more clearly, the bars may be divided into three equal parts, the first for the first *demi-coupé*, the second for the second, and the third for the two *pas marchés*, which should not require more time than a *demi-coupé*.

But it should be observed that in making this last *pas* the heel must be lowered to the ground, to enable the knee to be bent in preparation for another *pas*. To make my explanation easier of comprehension I shall now describe the manner of making this *pas* that its execution may not be hindered.

Having then the left foot in front, let it support the weight of the body, and bring the right foot close to the left in the first position. Bend the left knee without letting the right foot touch the ground. When the left knee is sufficiently bent, move the right foot to the fourth position front, at the same time rising *sur la demi-pointe*, straightening both knees and bringing both legs together as shown in the fourth part of the *demi-coupé* (Fig. 26), called the equilibrium or balance. Then lower the right heel to the ground to keep the body steady and at the same time bend the right knee, without allowing the left foot to touch the ground, and move the latter to the fourth position front and rise on the left *demi-pointe*, straightening both knees and bringing both legs together in the balance. Then execute two *pas marchés sur la demi-pointe*, the first with the right foot, the second with the left, lowering the left heel to the ground after the second, in order to have the body firmly placed ready to begin another *pas de menuet*.

In the execution of *demi-coupés*, take care to open the knees and turn the toes well outwards, but the best manner of acquiring facility of execution is to perform several in succession, which accustoms one to perform them without difficulty. These two movements should succeed each other with the body at an equal height, but after the second *demi-coupé* do not lower the heel to the ground, to avoid interrupting the sequence of the two *pas marchés;* in the last, that performed by the left foot, the heel must be lowered in readiness to begin another *pas de menuet*.

No one should attempt to perform this *pas* backwards or sideways, until he or she is quite certain of the *pas* forwards. The *pas de menuet* backwards is almost the same as that forwards, except that on the completion of the first *demi-coupe* with the right foot, you leave the left leg extended in front, and while bending the right knee in preparation for the second *demi-coupé* you bring the left heel close to the right, where it remains while you bend to the fullest extent, to step back upon it in order to rise. This affords you more ease to do it well, whereas, if you stepped back before the completion of your bending, you would never rise so well and the knees would always appear bent. These observations are very important, especially in regard to dancing the *Menuet* to perfection.

As for the *pas de menuet* sideways, moving to the right, which may be termed the open *pas de menuet*, because the first step is made in the second position, it is executed similarly to that backwards and differs from it in direction alone. The *pas de menuet* backwards is made by retiring on a straight line; the *pas de menuet* sideways by moving on a horizontal line and to the right.

There is also another way, moving to the left side, which is different in that it is crossed, although made in the same line but returning from right to left. This is the manner. The body being supported on the left foot, you bend the left knee, then cross the right foot in the fifth position front and rise on the right *demi-pointe;* the left following extended at its side, with both heels close together. Then lower the right heel to the ground and bend the right knee with the toe turned well outwards. Afterwards, slide the left foot to the second position and rise *sur les demi-pointes*, the legs being well extended and the heels off the ground. Then execute two *pas marchés sur la demi-pointe*, that with the right foot being crossed in the fifth position back, that with the left being opened to the second position, gently lowering the heel to the ground, which makes a kind of third movement when done well and gives more vivacity to your *Menuet*.

When you have practised the execution of these different *pas*, you make a particular figure with them which is called the *Menuet*, which I shall explain in the following chapter.

CHAPTER XXII

Of the Menuet and the Manner of Dancing it Correctly

THE *Menuet* has become the most fashionable dance, due to the facility with which it may be performed and to the easy figure now in use, which we owe to Monsieur Pécourt, who gave the *Menuet* much of its present grace by changing the form S, which was the principal figure, to a Z, in which the steps keep the dancers in the same relation to the figure, as demonstrated in the course of this chapter.

After you have made the customary bows before dancing and the second one being finished, you must execute a *pas de menuet* in returning to the place whence you made your first bow, tracing a quarter-circle as shown in Fig. 27 (1), which brings you up to your lady, to whom you present your hand as shown in Fig. 27 (2), which shows that the gentleman's hand should support the lady's from underneath and hers should rest on his.

Afterwards you both execute two *pas de menuet* forwards, holding hands in the manner described (see Fig. 28).

Fig. 29 shows that the gentleman makes a *pas de menuet* backwards, to allow the lady to pass by him, and then another sideways, at the end of which he leaves hold of her hand

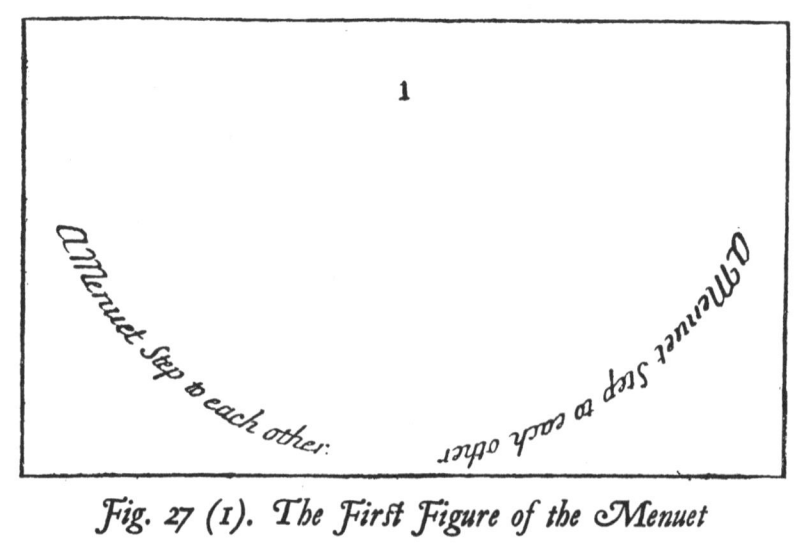

Fig. 27 (1). The First Figure of the Menuet

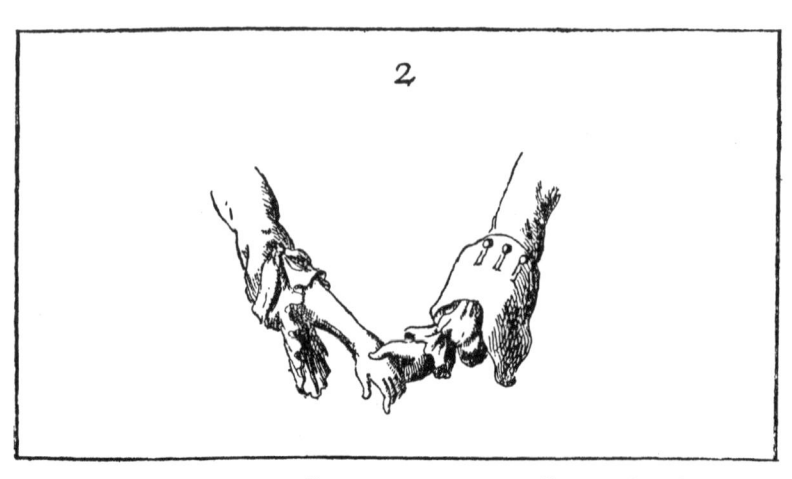

Fig. 27 (2). The Manner of taking Hands

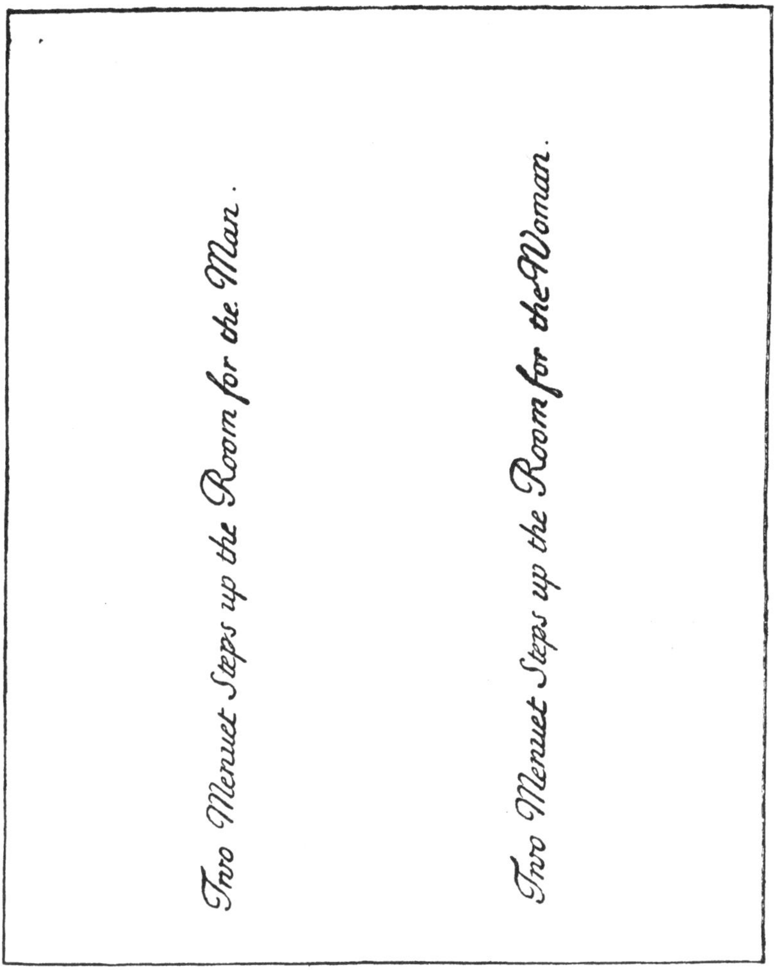

Two Menuet Steps up the Room for the Man.

Two Menuet Steps up the Room for the Woman.

Fig. 28. The Second Figure of the Menuet

and makes one forwards and the lady makes one going down, as explained in this written plan (see Fig. 29), which traces the path to be described and names the *pas*. Afterwards, each executes a *pas de menuet* sideways to the right, at an oblique angle which brings them opposite each other by the quarter turn made at the first step of the *pas de menuet* sideways, as described. But, in making this *pas*, you both shade your right shoulders a little, turn your heads slightly to your left and look at each other, which manner should be retained throughout the dance; but, above all, no affectation.

To continue the figure as represented in Fig. 30, two *pas de menuet* must be made sideways to the left, keeping the body upright. But, in making your next two *pas de menuet* forwards, keep your right shoulders shaded, the gentleman always allowing the lady to pass on his right, both looking at each other. To shade the shoulder is to draw it slightly backwards so that the top half of the body is almost facing. Nevertheless, continue to make your steps forwards as shown in Fig. 30, which is the principal figure of the *Menuet*. But when you have made five or six turns in succession you must, from one corner or other of the room, and looking at each other, each present your right hand as you advance.

In order that you may understand this the better, when you are giving hands, that is at the end of your last *pas* returning to the left, you raise your right arm sideways, in a line with the chest, with the palm downwards as shown in Fig. 31. The head being turned to the right and both looking at each other, you make a little upward movement of the wrist and elbow with a slight inclination of the head on presenting the hand, and, still looking at each other, you make a complete circle as shown in Fig. 31.

Having left hold of the right hand, you go forwards, making a half turn to present the hand again, in this case the left, observing the same ceremony as for the right, as shown in Fig. 32.

When you leave hold of the left hand, you must make a *pas de menuet* sideways to the right, obliquely backwards as shown by the sign 4, which brings you again into your principal figure, which you continue for three or four turns.

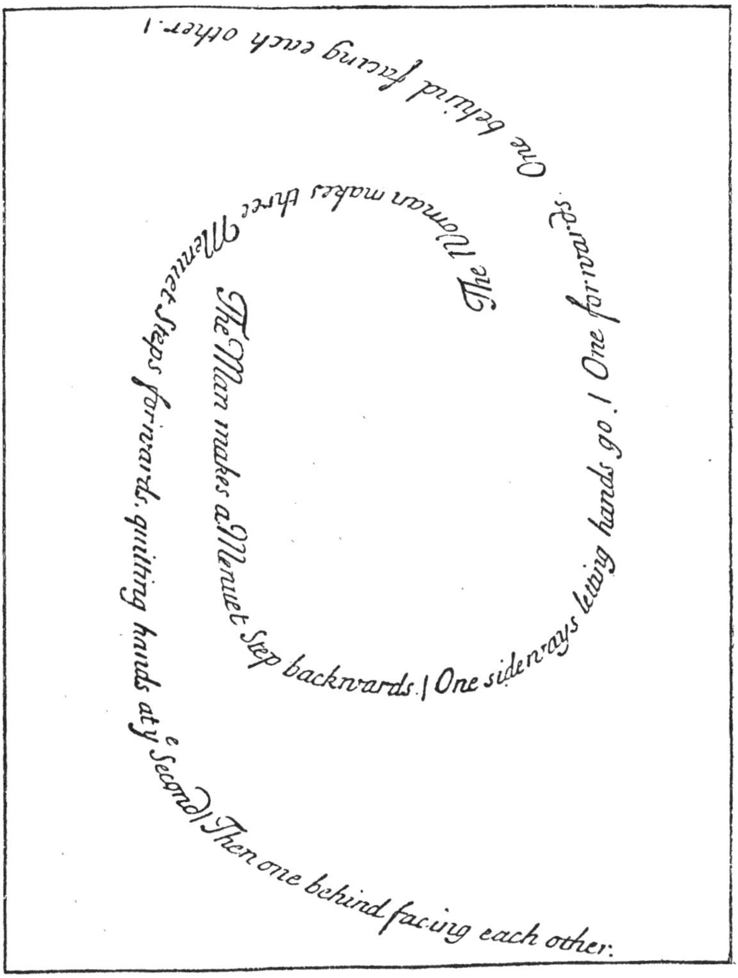

The Man makes a Menuet Step backwards. | One sideways letting hands go. | One forwards. One behind facing each other. | The Woman makes three Menuet Steps forwards, quitting hands at ye Second | Then one behind facing each other:

Fig. 29. The Third Figure of the Menuet

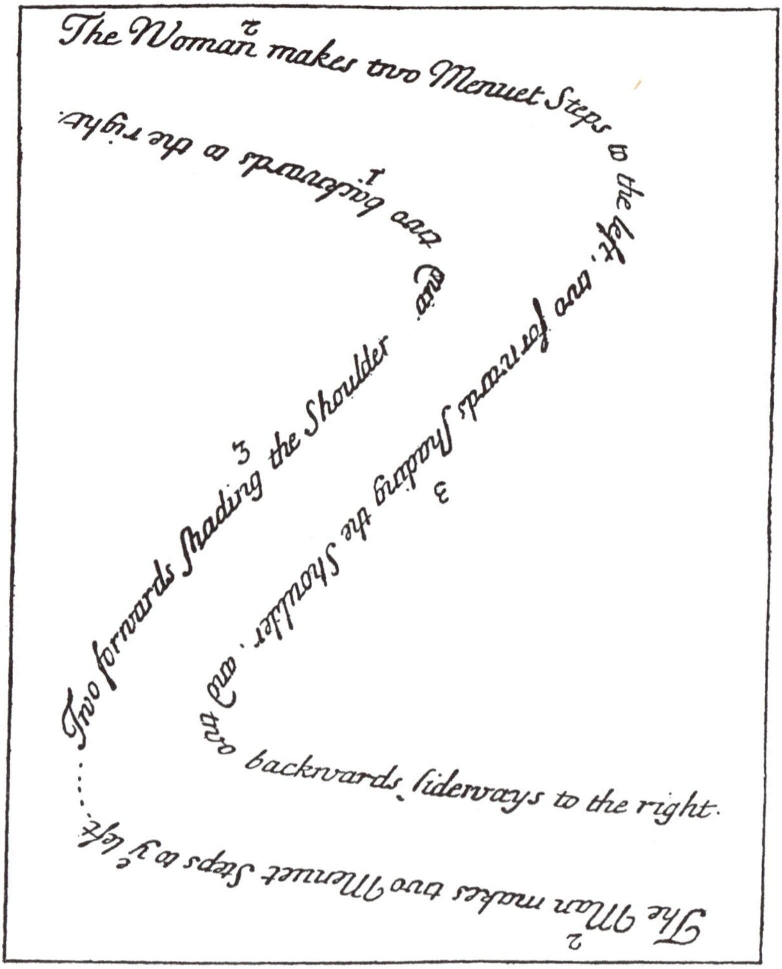

The Woman makes two Menuet Steps to the left, and two backwards to the right.

Two forwards shading the Shoulder and two forwards shading the Shoulder, and two backwards, sideways to the right.

The Man makes two Menuet Steps to y^e left.

Fig. 30. The Fourth and Principal Figure of the Menuet

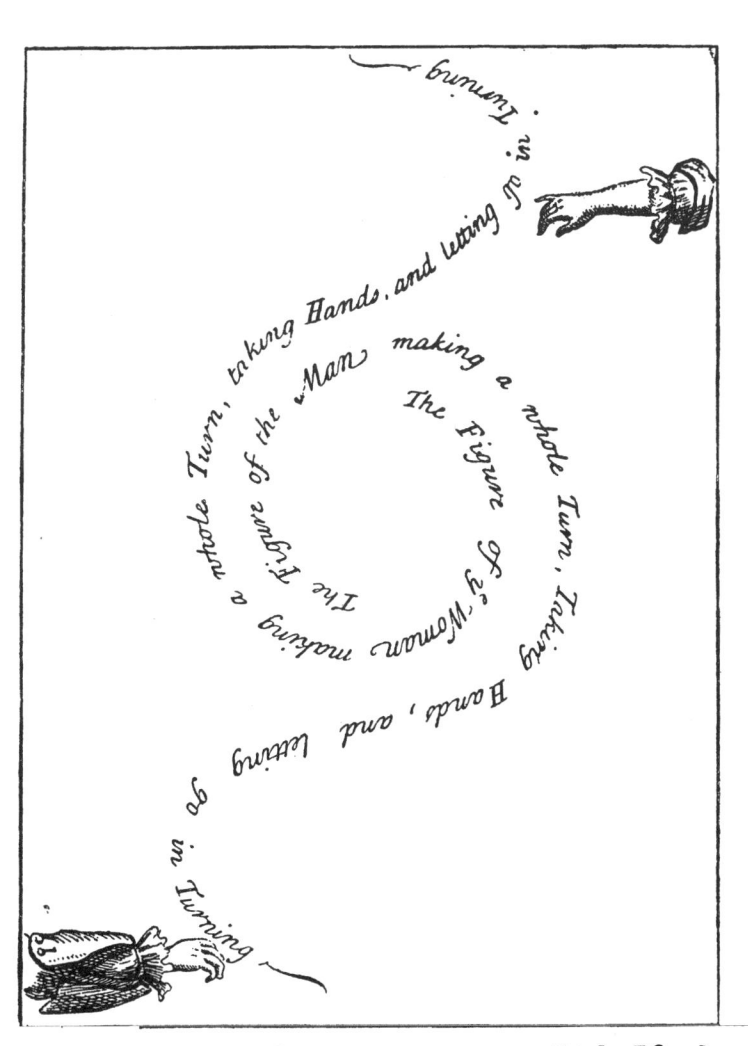

Fig. 31. The Fifth Figure—presenting Right Hands

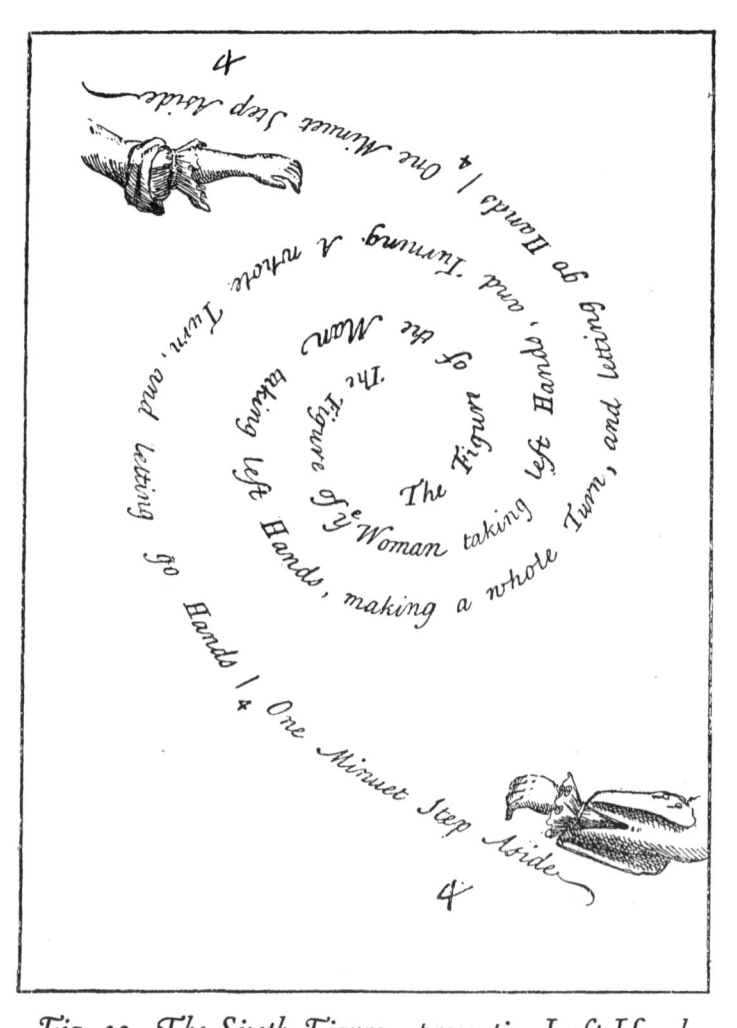

Fig. 32. The Sixth Figure—presenting Left Hands

Then you present both hands, raising both arms to the height of the breast and inclining the body as shown in Fig. 33.

In presenting hands to the lady, following the manner I have endeavoured to express in Fig. 33, and when you take hands, you make a turn or two. But the gentleman makes a *pas de menuet* backwards, bringing the lady with him, withdrawing his left hand only in order to take off his hat at the same time. The *pas de menuet* completed, he carries his right foot to the second position, and they both make the same bows as before they danced.

I do not say that if a *Menuet* be danced a little longer it becomes displeasing, but, in my opinion, although it may seem arbitrary to fix a limit, it is both reasonable and becoming, for however good the dancing, the figure is always the same, hence the shorter the *Menuet* the better.

But when one has come to dance it well, various graces may be introduced into it from time to time, as I shall explain in the following chapter.

CHAPTER XXIII

Of the Graces that may be Introduced into the Menuet and the Care that should be taken to Dance it uniformly

ALTHOUGH, in the opinion of many, the simpler the *Menuet* the better, I have seen certain embellishments introduced by which it was made more pleasing and graceful, and these are so much used that I feel called upon to tell you how to do them, that you may employ them either in presenting hands or in other parts of the dance.

I shall begin with the *pas de menuet* forwards. Having, at the conclusion of this, the weight of the body on the left foot, bring the right foot to it, then bend and rise immediately. Afterwards slide the right foot to the fourth position front, rise on the right *demi-pointe*, spring on the left foot and continue your *pas de menuet*.

But to accustom yourself to perform this with ease, practise several alternately with a *pas de menuet*, and, when you have acquired a certain facility of execution, use this *pas* in appropriate places where it will achieve the most graceful effect. For instance, in presenting hands when you have finished your *pas de menuet*, coming from the left side and going towards the lady, you raise your right arm, as I have already said, to present hands. But, in this case, instead of making a *pas de menuet* forwards, you make the *pas* described, which should be well sustained, allowing the head and body to make a slight inclination so that they will recover their previous position on making a *jeté échappé*. Then continue your *pas de menuet* according to the figure to be performed.

I call this spring a *jeté échappé*, because when you have made the slow *pas* and risen on the right *demi-pointe*, with both legs extended, the right knee immediately bends and consequently transfers the weight of the body to the left leg, which moves gently forwards, alighting on its foot, so that this movement cannot be termed otherwise, since the spring is but half executed.

This *pas* can be used in another place, that is, when you pass by each other during the *pas de menuet* forwards.

It can be used on yet another occasion, when you dance with a person who executes three *pas de menuet* to your two, so that you find yourself making your *pas de menuet* sideways to the right, while your partner is going forwards. Therefore, to conform to the figure, you make this slow *pas* going to the right, bending both knees, then rising on the left foot, at the same time sliding the right to the second position. Transfer the weight of the body to the right foot and rise *sur les demi-pointes*. But, owing to the position of the body and this rising, the left leg follows, allowing the right heel to rest on the ground with the knee bent. By this movement the left leg is obliged to cross in front of the right, making a *jeté échappé*. Then you make your *pas de menuet* going to the left side, which restores both of you to your proper places in the figure.

There are some persons who use this *pas* while passing

Fig. 33

each other, but it must not be repeated too often, for that would look affected.

Having discussed the feeling and intelligence necessary to dance well, there still remain two more essentials, the ear and the arms. In regard to the first, the pupil who has little ear for cadence must devote himself to marking the time when his master teaches him, and be instructed in this particular, that he may come to hear and understand that cadence which is the soul of dancing and the acquisition of which often depends only on a little application.

I have already stated that the *pas de menuet* is performed to two bars of triple time, hence there is a true and a false cadence. The true is the first, the false the second. But, as there are eight or twelve bars in a *menuet* strain, every first bar is the true cadence and the last the false. This cadence is marked by beating the right hand against the left, and the false by raising the hand, both cadences being of equal duration.

But the foot acts contrary to the hand because you rise on the right *demi-pointe* at the same time you clap, hence you must bend the knees at the end of the last bar in order to be ready to rise when you beat the hands. The cadence is expressed in two ways in dancing, that is, the *pas* which consist of sinking and rising are raised in the cadence; but those which consist of jumping fall in it. Hence the movements should be taken a little in advance, that is, you must bend at the end of the last bar in order to be able to rise if required.

CHAPTER XXIV

Of the Carriage of the Arms in the Menuet

THE manner of moving the arms gracefully in the *Menuet* is as important as the execution of the *pas*, because the arms move with the body and are its principal ornament.

Therefore, the arms should be held at the sides of the body as shown in Fig. 34, the hands being neither open nor closed, because should the thumb press against one of the fingers, this fixed position would stiffen the upper joints and prevent the arms from moving with the smoothness proper to the occasion.

Having the arms disposed as directed, you allow them to fall to the bottom of your coat pockets as you make your first *demi-coupé* with the right foot, the hands turned inwards (see Fig. 35).

But as you execute the second movement with the left foot, the elbow bends slightly so that the hands are imperceptibly raised as shown in Fig. 36. Afterwards you open them very gently, gracefully extending them until you have concluded your *pas de menuet;* and do likewise in every *pas de menuet* you perform, whether it be forwards, backwards, or sideways.

I must observe that although I have made use of three different illustrations, that is merely for the better explanation of the different positions, and to cause the reader to appreciate all the *temps*. Hence, all these successive movements make but one, and are all included in a *pas de menuet*.

I have seen many persons make *balancés* in dancing the *Menuet*, when the arms are disposed differently than for other *pas*. The arms should be raised to the height of the hip, and in making your first *balancé*, which is done with the right foot, the left arm is in opposition and carried slightly forwards, also the shoulder, while the right arm and shoulders are drawn backwards. At the same time the head is inclined a little. But at the second *balancé* both the head and arms resume their previous positions.

As for ladies, who are only to use their arms in the *Menuet* when presenting hands, it is sufficient if at the first *balancé* they shade the right shoulder, which brings the left forwards in opposition to the foot, and make a slight inclination of the head, which affords an infinite grace to this step. But, above all, beware of affectation.

During the whole *Menuet* it is sufficient if the lady hold her head erect and her body upright, avoiding any suggestion

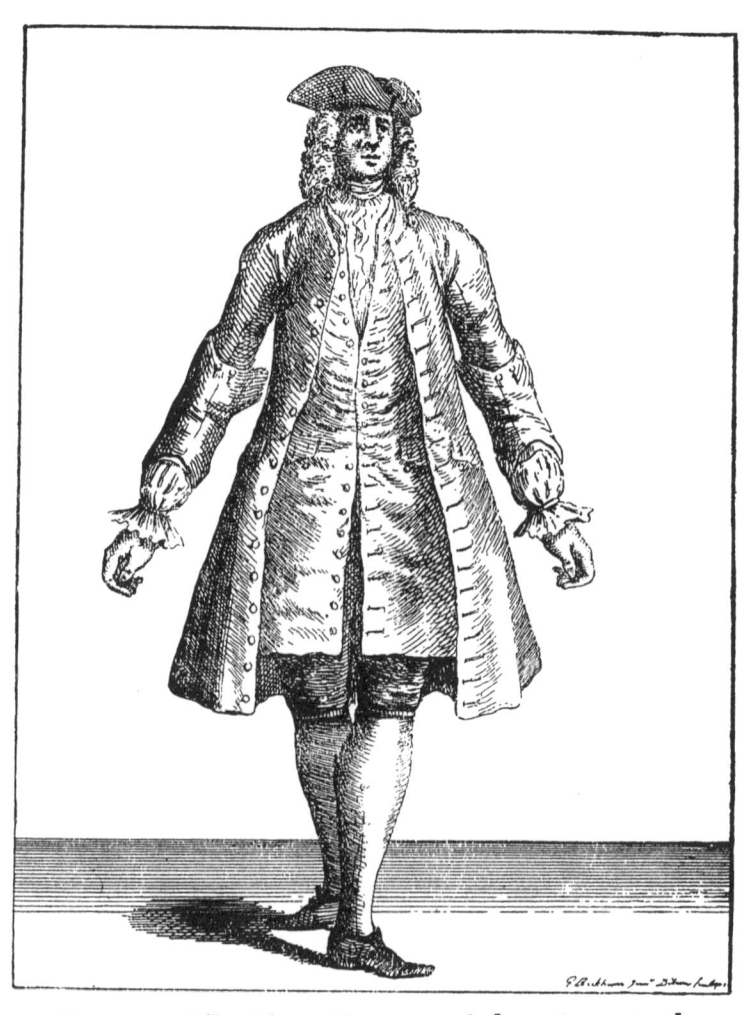

Fig. 34.—*The First Position of the Arms in the Menuet*

Fig. 35.—*The Second Position of the Arms in the Menuet*

Fig. 36.—The Third Position of the Arms in the Menuet

of stiffness, with the shoulders well back, which makes the breast fuller and gives more grace to the body. The arms are held extended at the sides so that the elbows almost touch the hips; but all must appear easy and natural.

To make my meaning plain, look at Fig. 37, which represents the deportment to be observed by a lady when dancing. She holds her skirt between the thumb and first finger, the arms extended at the sides, the hands turned outwards, without spreading the dress or squeezing it. In regard to her manner of dancing, it is the same as for the gentleman, such as shading the shoulder both in *pas* made sideways and in those made forwards; while in the presenting of hands, this, like the graces I have described, is the same for the one sex as for the other.

CHAPTER XXV

Of the Contretemps of the Menuet and the Manner of Performing it.

THE *contretemps* is made instead of a *pas de menuet*, but for some time this *pas* has been seldom used in the ordinary *Menuet*, since *Passepieds* and figured *Menuets* came into fashion. It is true that these dances have many graces owing to the variety of their figures and the different steps of which they composed, and since the *contretemps* forms part of their construction I shall describe the manner of its execution according to the rules of the art.

But to perform it well, you must first understand the formation of the *pas*. It contains three different kinds of *sauts* or hops. One is made before the *pas*, the second after the *pas*, and the third during the *pas*.

The first occurs when you have concluded your *pas de menuet*. As you finish it with the left foot, you transfer the weight of the body to it and bring the right to the first position. Then you bend the left knee and rise on it with a little hop which is commonly termed *sauter à cloche pied*, and that is the hop before the *pas*.

Fig. 37.—A Lady holding her Dress to Dance

The second occurs when, leaving the weight of the body on the left foot, you bend the left knee a second time, and, keeping the knee bent, slide the right foot to the fourth position front and rise on it with a little hop. This is the hop after the *pas*.

The third and last occurs when, having the weight of the body on the right foot, you bend the right knee and bring the left foot to the right foot, then, rising, you pass it gently forwards and fall on it with a hop. This is the hop during the *pas*.

But when you thoroughly understand these three *temps*, you do them in succession so as to execute the complete *pas*.

To accustom yourself to perform it with ease, you should do this *pas* alternately with a *pas de menuet* and execute several in succession. This will not only make you proficient but afford you a certain lightness, so that as your mastery increases you will gradually be able to soften your movements.

Ladies perform the *contretemps* in the same manner, save that the hop should be less pronounced, both for the sake of decorum and because it would be out of keeping for them. And when you dance a *Passepied* or figured *Menuet* with a lady, you must soften your *contretemps* to agree with her own quiet manner and to achieve that harmony between you which contributes so much to the beauty of dancing.

Moreover, the hopped *contretemps* is only suitable for young persons or those of medium height. Those who are tall should make a *temps de courante* and a *demi-jeté* as I explained in the manner of taking hands, because it is not agreeable for tall persons to hop and fret themselves in figured dances, where all the movements are soft and graceful and do not detract from that graceful manner so much esteemed by, and so characteristic of, our nation; which cannot be said of the many *contre-danses* lately introduced into France and which are not to the taste of lovers of fine dancing.

Indeed there are many lacking in both design and taste,

because the figures are always the same and without any fixed steps. The whole aim of these *contre-danses* is for the performers to twist and turn their bodies, to stamp their feet as if they wore sabots, and to assume attitudes contrary to decorum.

I am told that these dances please everyone because a great many can dance at once. Is it not possible for many people to dance together, using graceful and refined steps common to German dances, such as I have observed in Germany? For, though they change their movements, they maintain a certain order which prevents confusion, especially among people of distinction. These dances can be arranged for many people and can be done to different kinds of music, such as an air in quick duple time or the *Menuet*; but I hope the masters who compose these dances will set them down by means of characters, that they may be performed according to the notation.

We see in *Branles* how each dancer leads in his turn, which does not occasion disorder as in a number of these *contre-danses* which I have seen danced by persons devoid of taste, all of which detracts from the pleasure to be derived from witnessing good dancing.

CHAPTER XXVI

Of the Courante in General

FORMERLY, the *Courante* was much in fashion, and as it is a very solemn dance with a nobler style and grander manner than the others, is very varied in its figures, and has dignified and distinguished movements, Louis XIV., of happy memory, was pleased to prefer it.

For after the *Branles* with which, as I have already stated, all Court Balls were and are still begun, His Majesty danced the *Courante*. Indeed, he danced it better than any member of his Court and with a quite unusual grace.

But what testifies still more to the attachment and

preference he had for the dance is that, despite the weighty affairs which continually occupied the mighty conqueror, he never failed to set aside some hours each day for the practice of it, throughout all the twenty-two years that Monsieur Beauchamps had the honour to instruct him in this noble exercise.

Hence the dance I mention, as avowed by the most able masters, has always been regarded as one very necessary to know how to dance well, which has determined me to give a brief description of its principal movements, which will enable you to dance other dances easily; this shall be proved from the manner in which it is done.

After you have made the customary bows before dancing, as I have already described, on rising from your second bow, you leave the weight of the body on the right foot and carry the left to the fourth position front. Then you transfer the weight of the body to the latter, and, presenting your hand to the lady, you execute a *temps de courante*. Afterwards you begin the *pas de courante* with a *demi-jeté* on the left foot and then a *coupé* on the right, which concludes the *pas*. (Observe the difference between the *temps de courante* and the *pas de courante*). Then you begin another with the right foot, making a *demi-jeté* with this foot and a *coupé* with the left.

But as all these different *pas* lead you into a symmetrical figure which forms an ellipse, at this last *coupé* you begin again, making a step with the left foot and a *temps de courante* or *pas grave* with the right, and again continue the *demi-jetés* and *coupés*, which are to be repeated throughout the dance.

But as I did not undertake to describe the figures of dances, I shall leave masters to instruct their pupils in them, the more readily since the dance is no longer in vogue, any more than the *Dauphine*, the *Duchesse*, and the *Bocanne*, which were very beautiful dances. Those persons who are curious regarding them must study the characters by which they have been set down.

As for the dances in present use, the figures and steps of which are so varied that they demand some application, I shall give you the easiest way to perform all these different *pas* in turn, so that masters may have the pleasure of seeing their pupils profit still more by their lessons through acquaintance with this easy method.

To see a gradual improvement in our pupils is one of the greatest pleasures that our masters have. This is the sole aim of my treatise, and I dare to flatter myself that I have succeeded.

CHAPTER XXVII

Of the Temps de Courante, or Pas Grave

AS formerly the teaching of dancing began with the *Courante*, and since I have promised to proceed step by step, to be in order I shall commence with the *temps de courante* or *pas grave*, which is one of the first movements and the most graceful.

First, you must understand that the step is only called a *temps* because it consists of but one single step and movement. It retains the same value when used to form another step composed of several movements, such as a *pas de courante* or *pas de bourrée*. That is the difference between a *temps* and a *pas*.

But this *temps* is not employed solely in the *Courante*, but in all kinds of dances where it produces a good effect and affords grace to the body by its smooth and quiet movements, which must be attained if it is to be done well.

Let us suppose, then, that this *temps* is to be made with the right foot. Having the left foot foremost and supporting the weight of the body, and the right in the fourth position back, with the heel raised ready to move, you bend the knees and open the right foot sideways. Then you rise and, when the knees are straight, you slide the right foot to the fourth position front and transfer the weight of the body to it. But as the right foot slides forwards, the left knee bends and the heel rises, thus throwing the weight of the body easily on to the right foot, and immediately you rise on the right *demi-pointe*. Afterwards you lower the right heel to the ground, which finishes your *temps de courante* or *pas grave*. The body being at rest, due to the whole of the foot being placed on the ground, from thence you may make another with the left foot, observing the same precautions; and to become accustomed to them you should practise several, first with one foot and then with the other.

I have seen many persons make this movement from the first position and with a good effect. But it seemed to me to be more difficult so, because, when the body is supported on one foot, the rear foot follows and meets the other in the first position (without touching the ground), when you bend and rise immediately without moving the foot until the knees are straight. Then you lower to the ground the heel of the foot on which you rose, and its knee bends in proportion as you slide the foot that was off the ground to the fourth position front, which is the extent of your step. But when the foot is completely passed and the heel lowered to the ground, the body rests easily upon it, and you rise *sur la demi-pointe* and afterwards lower the heel to the ground, which completes the step.

This step can also be made *de côté*, when it is begun from a different position, because it is generally made after a *pas de bourrée dessus et dessous*, which finishes in the third position. Therefore it is from this position that you move after bending both knees, without changing your position until you have risen; then you slide the front foot.

For instance, suppose you have made a *pas de bourrée dessus et dessous* with the left foot, going sideways to the right, the right foot will be found in the third position front. Then you bend both knees, and, having straightened them, you slide the right foot sideways to the second position and transfer the weight of the body to it, which concludes your step. But, if you wish to execute this movement with the other foot, you must transfer the weight of the body to the left foot, and, having completed your *pas de bourrée*, you bend both knees, then straighten the right, sliding the left sideways to the second position. The weight of the body is transferred to it by your rising on the left *demi-pointe*, and immediately lowering the heel to the ground, which finishes the step. The body being placed in equilibrium, you can perform what steps you please and with either foot.

There are other steps which we only call *temps*, but which must not be confounded with these; for, although their first movements are made in the same manner, they do not end like the others, because this *temps* is a bend and a rise, and you open the foot to the side without a slide, which is the difference between them. Since you will find many of them placed differently in *L'Aimable Vainqueur*,[1] this has induced me to furnish you with a clear description of them.

For instance, having the weight of the body supported on the left foot in the fourth position, you bend the left knee, then straighten it, opening the right foot sideways to the second position, placing only the toe on the ground; and you wait a bar before commencing another step, which produces a most graceful effect. For if this movement be executed properly, with the body resting in an easy position, it is most graceful; especially when succeeding another livelier step which, owing to the contrast, appears still quicker, and contributes so much to the beauty of dancing, when you know how to employ it appropriately in all these different movements and steps, for it adds nobility to the slow steps and vivacity to the quick ones.

[1] See Footnote on page 85.

CHAPTER XXVIII

Of the Pas de Bourrée and Fleuret

THE *pas de bourrée* is composed of two movements; that is, a *demi-coupé*, a *pas marché sur la demi-pointe* and a *demi-jeté*, which makes the second movement and is the extent of the *pas*. I call it a *demi-jeté* because it is only half a bound, and, since the *pas* is a flowing one, for that reason its last movement must not be marked too strongly. As this *pas* requires a certain ease of movement in the instep, particularly in the case of ladies, it has been largely replaced by the *fleuret*, a very similar *pas* which contains three steps and only one movement. It is a simple *pas* and easily learned. To know its construction is to be able to perform it immediately. It consists of a *demi-coupé* and two *pas marchés sur la demi-pointe*.

Although I have explained the manner of executing a *demi-coupé* when dealing with the construction of the *pas de menuet*, nevertheless, to make you understand it better, I shall say that when you wish to perform a *fleuret*, being in the fourth position, left foot front and supporting the weight of the body, you bring the right foot to the first position without touching the ground, then bend both knees, which is termed *plier sous soi*. But do not move the right foot to the fourth position front until you have made your bend. As you move the foot forwards rise *sur la demi-pointe*, then make two *pas marchés sur la demi-pointe*, that is, the first with the left, the second with the right, lowering the heel of the latter at the last, so that the body is firm, ready to repeat the *pas* or begin another, according to the requirements of the dance. But to acquire facility in executing this *pas*, it is well to perform many in succession with each foot in turn, so that you are equally proficient with either.

Hence, if you be asked of how many steps a *fleuret* is composed, you can reply three: that is, a *demi-coupé* and two *pas marchés sur la demi-pointe*.

The *fleuret* can be made similarly *en arrière* or *de côté*, the positions only being different according to the figure of the dance, whether it be *en tournant* or going *de côté*.

For instance, if you wish to make a *pas de bourrée* or *fleuret dessus et dessous* in returning to the left side, and supposing the right foot to be in the first position, you bend the left knee, opening the knees, then, keeping the knees bent, you cross the right foot in the fifth position front and rise *sur la demi-pointe*. Then you open the left foot to the second position and cross the right in the fifth position back, which completes the *pas*.

Sometimes, this *pas* is made *dessous et dessus*, which is the same, save that the *demi-coupé* is crossed in the fifth position back and the third step is made in the fifth position front, which is the whole difference.

There are others made *de côté*, shading the shoulder, as follows : Suppose the weight of the body to be supported on the left foot, you bend the left knee and bring the right foot in the first position, but without letting it touch the ground. Then you open the right foot to the second position, rising *sur les demi-pointes*, and drawing the right shoulder backwards. The left foot follows the right and passes to the third position back, the knees straight and the feet *sur les demi-pointes*, and for the third step you slide the right foot to the fourth position front and lower the heel to the ground, which completes the *pas*. The body so supported on the right foot, you can bend the right knee and make this *pas* with the left foot according to the same rules. These *pas de bourrée* are used at the end of the *Bretagne* and in many other genteel dances, and when these *pas* are well done they are most graceful.

This *pas* can be made in another manner, termed *pas de bourrée ouvert*. For instance, supposing you have the feet in the first position, with the right off the ground ; you bend the left knee, open the right foot to the second position and rise *sur la demi-pointe*. This draws the left foot to the first position, at the same time the right is lowered to the ground. Then you open the left foot to the second position, lowering the foot to the ground, heel first. And when the body rests on that foot you rise *sur la demi-pointe*, which draws the right foot so that it slides to the third position back, which concludes the *pas*.

But if you wish to make another with the left foot, you must lower the right heel to the ground, bend the right knee and open the left foot to the second position in the same manner, and learn to do it equally well with either foot.

This *pas* can be executed in still another manner. Having made your first step, which is a *demi-coupé*, and the weight of the body being supported on the left foot, you bend the left knee, meanwhile you beat the right foot, which is off the ground, against the left instep, open it to the second position and rise *sur la demi-pointe*, otherwise you continue your *pas de bourrée* as described.

There is yet another manner called *pas de bourrée emboité*, in which there is a pause at the second step, which I shall now explain. The *demi-coupé* must be made backwards by carrying the foot to the fourth position, in the second step you carry it quickly to the third position, and there you wait a little with the knees straight and the feet *sur les demi-pointes*. Then you slide the front foot to the fourth position front, which movement is made by bending the knee of the rear foot, which throws the weight of the body on the front foot, and this is the extent of the step.

This *pas* is done to all manner of airs and made in all kinds of figures, and, because it is easy and flowing, it can be made *en tournant* like the preceding one; but as it is the masters' duty to instruct their pupils in the regularity of the dances they teach them, I shall content myself with explaining how to execute these different *pas*.

There is another step of the same kind termed *pas de bourrée vite*, or *pas de bourrée* of four steps; but as I have consulted very skilful masters regarding the manner of executing these steps and on the names proper to them and find them divided in their opinions, I shall not form a decision myself, but leave all parties to call them by whatever names they think fit. I shall only say that the true *pas de bourrée* is the one I described first, and the *fleuret* the second. Thus the true *pas de bourrée* contains two movements, and the *fleuret* one only. But, in my opinion, I can give the *pas de bourrée vite* the name of *pas de bourrée doublé*, because it begins with a *demi-coupé*, then two *pas marchés sur la demi-pointe* and a *demi-jeté*, which completes the *pas*. Hence this *pas* can be said to consist of a *fleuret* and a *demi-jeté*.

But as I only proposed to give the manner of executing these different *pas*, I shall not discuss their etymology, because the majority of these different *pas* derive their nomenclature from the different dances common to out provinces, which have conferred on them all those properties which art permits and whose names they bear.

F

For instance, the *pas de rigaudon* is taken from the *Rigaudon*, a dance very popular in Provence and one which the inhabitants of that district dance habitually; and in each canton the dance varies, as I observed when I was in that country.

The *Gavotte* comes originally from the Lyonnais and the Dauphiné, and it is from these districts that we have taken the numerous *contretemps* we have in dancing, introduced by the pains of the many great masters we have had, to whom all credit is due for having given these steps all the grace they possess to-day, which has brought such brilliance and good taste to this art.

The *Bourrée* comes from Auvergne, the *Menuet* from Poitou and Anjou. The *Passepied*, which is lighter, is the dance most favoured in Brittany, although, according to some historians, it is a very ancient dance. And so with many others, whose origin I shall not attempt to give.

There is another *pas* known as a *fleuret* which can be performed in two ways, but as I have not encountered it in Ballroom Dancing I shall not explain it, having only seen it cited in connection with a *pas de bourrée* containing but one movement, called a *fleuret*. That is why I reserve this explanation for another volume, which will contain all the different *pas de ballet*.

CHAPTER XXIX

Of Coupés of Different Kinds

THE ordinary *coupé* is composed of two steps, that is, a *demi-coupé* and a *pas glissé*.[1] But in case the term "slide" should not be understood by all those learning to dance, particularly young persons whose high spirits makes them forgetful of the lessons taught them by their masters, I shall make the following observation: A sliding step is made by passing the foot gently forwards so that it hardly touches the ground. Hence it must be understood that this

[1] Sliding step.

step is slower than one in which the foot is moved forwards without touching the ground. Thus a slide implies a very slow step, which contributes in some degree to the perfection of the *coupé*. The bend should be made at the proper moment, the rising being made in cadence and sustained with grace. I say that the bend should be made correctly, so that you bend at the end of the bar to rise again on the next beat, which in dancing is termed cadence.

Therefore, to begin this *pas* with the right foot, the left foot must be foremost and supporting the weight of the body. Then bring the right foot against it in the first position, bend both knees equally and, keeping them bent, pass the right foot to the fourth position front and rise *sur la demi-pointe*, straightening the knees. Lower the right heel to the ground, then the knee bends, but the left foot slides forwards to the fourth position and the weight of the body is transferred to it, which completes the *coupé*.

Others perform this *pas* differently, that is, having made the *demi-coupé* and risen *sur la demi-pointe*, they slide the foot to the fourth position as they rise, the toe pointed to the ground in passing and the leg well extended, and as the left foot moves forward the right knee bends and through this movement throws the weight of the body on the left foot, which concludes the *pas*. Both ways are good, but I think the first is easier, because the body is firmer, through resting on the right heel. This *pas* can be made *en arrière*, *de côté* and approximate positions according to the figure that is to be followed.

Though this *pas* is made in several ways, the change occurs only in the second step, because the first is always a *demi-coupé;* and, having many times explained the manner of making one, I shall not repeat it in the following *pas*, but merely state a *demi-coupé* with such a foot. *Coupés battus*, or beaten *coupés*, are made in ballroom dances; for instance, you make your *demi-coupé en avant* with the right foot and the left approaches the right, beats the calf and returns to the fourth position back. This *battement* or beating takes the same time as when you pass the foot forwards.

There are others in which the *demi-coupé* is made *en avant;*

for instance, if you make the *demi-coupé* with the right foot forwards, at the same time you rise on it the left foot makes a beat behind and in front and opens sideways, or remains in the air according to the *enchaînement* of the *pas*.

There are still others which end with an *ouverture de jambe*, or *tour de jambe*, and the leg remains in the air to make the next *pas* which follows, as the dance requires.

There is yet another kind of *coupé* called *glissade*, but it is used only to move sideways on a line taken to right or left. For instance, if you wish to make *glissades* to the right you must bend the left knee and make your *demi-coupé* with the right foot by opening it sideways to the second position; in rising on it, you simultaneously draw the left foot to the third position back, leaving the weight of the body on it, in order to make another with the right. Because it is usual to make three in succession, though only two go to a bar, hence they should be made together that by their connection they may follow one another.

They are also made in another manner though keeping to the same line of direction, but a *demi-jeté* is made in place of a *demi-coupé*, and the rear foot is drawn to the third position. But as three are likewise made in succession, at the first the foot is drawn behind, at the second brought in front, and at the third it finishes sometimes in front or with the heels together in the first position, and sometimes even in the fourth position front, according to the steps that follow. The last are the most brilliant, for their first movement is a small hop, but it is best to learn to do the first well, then the others will follow of their own accord.

CHAPTER XXX

Of Coupés of Movement

THIS *pas* is one of the most graceful and most brilliant of all the different *pas* that have been invented, by the variety of its movements which are slow and which tend to inculcate grace when you know how to do it well.

For this reason I shall give the manner of performing it with all the correctitude it should have. When you make your *demi-coupé*, if *en avant*, you bend very smoothly and rise on the foot you move forwards, the legs well extended. The weight of the body being transferred to the foremost foot draws the rear one to it, which is similarly extended. But, at the same time, the heel of the front foot is lowered to the ground and its knee bends, and the leg which is in the air opens a little to the side, and the knee which is bent, being straightened, throws that leg forwards, so that you fall on it with a half-bound or *demi-jeté*, which concludes the *pas*.

I say that it is varied by these movements, because it is composed of two steps only, each of which contains two different movements. The first is bending on one foot, passing the other forwards and rising on it, which must be done gracefully; the second is bending on that foot, and rising with more vivacity to fall on the other with a half-bound, which gives this *pas* its gaiety.

For those that make it *de côté* it is the same thing, except that the foot is carried to the fifth position in the *demi-coupé*, and to the second for the *demi-jeté*. Others take it from the first position and carry the foot sideways to the second position, rising on it, and at the same time lower the heel to the ground to bend on it; and then the *demi-jeté* is taken across to the fifth position, which concludes the step. There are many examples of this *pas* in *L'Aimable Vainqueur*[1], which is a very beautiful ballroom dance. They are used in different ways and so appropriately that the legs seem to express the notes, which proves that harmony, or rather that imitation of music in dancing, since the sweetness of its sounds ought to be expressed by easy and graceful steps.

[1] See Rameau (P.) *Abbrégé de la Nouvelle Méthode dans l'Art d'Ecrire ou de Tracer toutes sortes de Danses de Ville.* 1725. Part II, p. 39, for a stenochoregraphic notation of this dance.

And as this is one of the most pleasing *pas* and there is a manner of moving the arms gracefully when performing it, this will be found in Part II, Chapter X.

CHAPTER XXXI

Of the Pas Tombé and Pas de Gaillarde

THIS *pas* is very unusual in its manner of execution and, I believe, derives its name entirely from its construction, contrarwise to the others, the majority of which are based on other steps. But this is different from its first movement, for you must rise *sur la demi-pointe* and bend after the step, as will be seen from the following description.

For instance, suppose you wish to make a *pas tombé* with the right foot, having the weight of the body on the left foot and the feet apart in the second position. In rising on the left foot, the right leg follows; for the body, inclining to the left, draws the right foot behind in the fifth position, and, in placing the foot on the ground, its knee bends, which raises the left foot; but the right knee being straightened, forces you to fall on the left foot in the second position, which is a *demi-jeté*, for it is only half a bound.

This *pas* is not difficult of execution when one knows how to perform the movements properly. It is the strength of the instep and the inclination of the body that draw the legs; and the knees bend as if their strength failed them, which forces the heel of the right foot drawn behind to rest on the ground, when its knee bends under the weight placed upon it, and then rises like a compressed spring when released. Thus the knee by its extension throws the weight of the body on the left foot, which completes the step.

The description I have given of this *pas* is only to show its peculiarity and to afford a clear explanation of it, that it may be well done, because this *pas* is preceded by another and their combination leads to a change of name due to the formation of another *pas*.

For instance, it can be preceded by a *coupé*, or by a *temps grave*, and very often by a *pas assemblé*, or joined step, when it becomes a *pas de gaillarde*. Thus, the *pas de gaillarde* is composed of an *assemblé*, a *pas marché* and a *pas tombé*, which is the whole construction and is many times repeated in the dance which bears its name, which inclines me to think that that is the sole reason why it has been given the name *pas de gaillarde*.

However it may be, this *pas* is very graceful and justly maintained in use, and is introduced in many ballroom dances. This *pas* can be made *en avant* and *de côté* in the same manner.

I shall begin first with that made *en avant*. Having the left foot in the fourth position front and supporting the weight of the body, and the right heel off the ground ready to move, you bend the left knee and simultaneously the right foot rises. And in rising to make a bound the right crosses in the third position front. You come to the ground on both feet, with the knees straight, when the right foot, which was crossed in front, opens to the fourth position front. At the same time, you transfer the weight of the body to the right foot and rise on the right *demi-pointe*, which brings the left leg behind it. But no sooner does it touch the leg, than the foot is lowered to the ground and the weight of the body transferred to it, which forces the left knee to bend and the right leg to rise. But at this same moment the left knee, which is bent, in endeavour to straighten throws the weight of the body on the right foot, which comes to the ground with a bound termed a *jeté-chassé*; but in falling on the right foot the left rises, and the body being completely in equilibrium and supported on the right foot, you can make another similar *pas* with the left foot. An example of this is given at the beginning of the third strain of the *Bacchante*.

I find this *pas* most graceful when well done and it deserves every attention. It can also be made *de côté* on the same line, but differently from that *en avant*.

For instance, having the weight of the body on the left foot, you bend and rise with a jump, bringing the right foot to the left in the first position, and come to the ground *sur les demi-pointes*. But the weight of the body rests on the left foot, because, at the same time, you open the right sideways to the second position, rising upon it to make your *pas tombé*, which is the second part of the composition of the *pas de gaillarde*. But, as I have given a sufficiently extended description of the *pas tombé*, it seems to me needless to repeat it a second time. This *pas*, being always preceded by a *coupé*, produces a very good effect by the sustained movements that should be observed in its correct performance.

CHAPTER XXXII

Of Pirouettes

THE *Pirouette* is a *pas* which is made *sur place*, that is, it moves neither forwards nor backwards, but its property is to make the body turn on one foot or both, as on a pivot, whether for a quarter-turn or half-turn, according as the foot is crossed or the dance you are learning requires.

Suppose, therefore, it must be done with the right foot, and that you must only make a quarter-turn to the right, you bend the left knee, the right foot being off the ground, and, as the knee bends, the right foot describes a semi-circle, then, lowering the right toe behind the left foot in the third position, to rise *sur les demi-pointes*, you make a quarter-turn. Or, if you wish to make a half-turn, you cross the toe farther so that it is in the fifth position, whence, on rising, you make a half-turn.

It must also be observed that, when you rise, the foot which made the semi-circle and was placed behind in the third or fifth position, owing to the body's turning, changes its place though not its position, because the rear foot becomes the front foot. Because, when you raise the body in making a quarter-turn or half-turn, it forces the legs by its movement to change their place to keep their equilibrium, so that the rear foot changes its place as I have already said.

But when you have risen and made the quarter-turn or half-turn, the heel of the foot supporting the body must be lowered to the ground in readiness to make another. This *pas* is very pleasing when made carefully, and should be accompanied by a movement of the arms and graceful carriage of the head, which is so important to the perfection of this *pas*. This shall be explained in Part II, for this part deals only with the manner of forming *pas*, whereas the other will deal with the carriage of the arms according to the rules of the art.

But, as this *pas* is very graceful and demands some reflection to perform it properly, this has engaged me to make the following remarks, so that being instructed carefully you can execute it correctly.

First, in the *pirouette* where the body is supported on one foot only, the bend must be taken very smoothly, the body resting entirely on the foot of the bent leg, because that which traces the circle has only the toe on the ground, and serves, so to speak, as a guide for the body to turn on the same arc, and when you rise this should be done with the same smoothness with which you sank, for such movements are always the most graceful and the most pleasing.

It is made in another way where both knees are bent, as that placed at the beginning of the second part of the *Bacchante*.[1] This *pas* is very easy to perform, because it is nothing more than bending both knees

---

[1] See Rameau, *op. cit.*, Part II, p. 51, for a stenochoregraphic notation of this dance.

equally and rising in the same manner. For instance, the right foot being in the fourth position front, and the body supported on both feet, you bend both knees and rise, turning the body a quarter-turn to the left; and in the reverse direction if the left foot is foremost, that is to the right.

There is still another way, different from the preceding ones, which is done in this manner. Being in the second or fourth position, for it is taken equally from either, and the weight of the body supported on one foot, the toe of the other being on the ground, you bend both knees and rise with a hop on the foot supporting the body. But, in making the hop on the supporting foot, the other, the toe of which was placed on the ground, extends following the body in the turn it makes either to right or left. If you are to turn to the right side, you bend and hop on the left foot, and the right arm and leg extends, which makes you turn to the right; and you do the same with the other leg and foot, if you wish to turn to the left.

CHAPTER XXXIII

Of the Balancé

THE *Balancé* is a *pas* made *sur place* like the *pirouette*, but it is generally made to the presence, though it may be made *en tournant*; but, as it is only the body that turns, and no movement is made in the *pas*, I shall describe the manner of making it to the presence.

First, I shall say that it is composed of two *demi-coupés*, one *en avant* and one *en arrière*, that is, you bend in the first position and open the foot to the fourth position and rise on it. Then you lower the heel to the ground, and the foot that is off the ground follows that in front and on which you rose; then you bend the knee of the foot which made the first step, and, the other, being bent, steps in the fourth position back and you rise on it, which concludes the *pas*. But, as in making the first *demi-coupé* the shoulder is shaded and the head makes a slight movement, this gives grace to the *pas* as I shall explain, together with the manner of moving the arms, in Part II.

I have seen many persons make this *pas de côté* in the second position, but to my mind this method is not so graceful, because the body seems to sway; furthermore, the movements of the head and arms are not so becoming. For those that are made *en tournant* depend on the bend and the rise, taking count of the proportion of the *pas* and the position of the feet, so that the body retains its equilibrium, since all *pas* made *en tournant* are more difficult of execution than those executed *en avant*.

The *balancé* is a most graceful *pas* and used with all manner of music, although the two steps of which it is composed are raised equally, and for this reason it can be adapted to all kinds of time because it is the ear which indicates when a movement should be quickened or slowed.

This *pas* is used in both figured and ordinary *Menuets*, as well as in the *Passepied*. It is made in place of a *pas de menuet* and occupies the same time, therefore it should be made slowly so that its two steps occupy the same time as the four steps which make up the *pas de menuet*.

CHAPTER XXXIV

Of the Pas de Sissonne

HAVING explained the manner of executing the different *pas* which consist of bending and rising, I now pass to those whose movements require more strength, that is:

pas sautés or hopping steps; and since the *pas de sissonne* is one of the easiest, I shall begin with this to explain their manner of execution.

This *pas* includes two different ways of hopping: one consists in bending to hop, and coming to the ground with the knees bent; in the other case, the knees being bent, you rise with a hop. Hence, if you wish to make this *pas* with the right foot, having the body supported on the left foot, you bend the left knee, and the right foot, which is off the ground, opens sideways at the same time. But when you rise with a hop, it crosses in front of the left in the third position, so that you come to the ground on both feet. Having the knees bent, you rise with a hop and come to the ground on the right foot, which completes the *pas*.

This *pas* is made similarly *en arrière*, except that instead of the movement being made from back to front, it is done with the front foot, which passes behind as you come to the ground on both feet, rising on the foot that was passed backwards.

There are others made *sur place*, but at the second hop you rise on the rear foot; that is, you bend the left knee in hopping and come to the ground on both feet, and at the second hop you rise on the left foot and the right remains off the ground, ready to make another *pas*.

This *pas* is also made *en tournant*, the manner is the same as coming to the ground on both feet and rising on one foot, it is only the outline of the body that changes, for the legs, having to support the body, follow it in all its movements. Moreover, the master, guiding the pupil by the hand, will complete what this treatise has begun.

There are yet others which are done similarly, except that at the first hop you come to the ground on both feet, without bending the knees, but you bend them afterwards in readiness for the second hop, which may be termed *pas de sissonne coupée*, because there is a pause made to bend for the second hop. This *pas* is placed in different strains in *L'Aimable Vainqueur*. And since it is in slow triple time, this *pas* must be performed in that manner, because then it fills the bar and expresses the cadence better.

CHAPTER XXXV

Of the Pas de Rigaudon

THIS *pas* is very unusual in its construction. It is made *sur place* without going forwards, backwards, or sideways; and, if the feet make several different movements, it has a lively effect. Therefore it is used in airs of light duple time, such as *Bourrées, Rigaudons*, and so forth.

It is begun from the first position. You bend both knees equally and rise with a hop, at the same time opening the right foot sideways, with the knee straight, then the foot is returned to the first position. But no sooner is it placed on the ground than the left foot opens sideways without any movement of the knee; it is moved solely by the action of the hip, and immediately comes to the ground. The feet being on the ground, you bend both knees and rise with a hop, coming to the ground on both feet, which concludes the *pas*. Afterwards, you make a *pas en avant* or *de côté* as you please, but this is independent of the *pas de rigaudon* and employed simply to connect that *pas* with another, and render easier the execution of the succeeding *pas*.

All these different movements are performed in quick succession, so that they make but one *pas*, which is executed in one bar of duple time, as I have said already. Therefore all the care to be taken in regard to this *pas* consists in that the knees must be straight when you rise, while you should come to the ground, keeping the knees straight, *sur les demi-pointes*, which will make you appear lighter.

Although this *pas* is much used in Provence, I have seen it made a little differently in that country, where the dancers, instead of opening the legs sideways, pass them in front, crossing them a little; but this manner is not so graceful. Moreover, when you execute them with one leg in front, it looks as if you were about to kick your partner.

CHAPTER XXXVI

Of Jetés, or Demi-Cabrioles

AS the *jeté* has been mentioned in connection with several *pas*, without any definite instructions regarding its manner of execution having been given, I shall explain it in this chapter, following the order of *pas*, that is, to pass from the easier to the more difficult.

This type is only part of another *pas*, as I have said already, thus a single *jeté* cannot occupy a whole bar, so that two must be made in succession to be equal to another *pas*. But it is easily combined to form other *pas*, as we see at the end of the *Menuet* in the *coupé* of movement, *pas tombé*, the quick *pas de bourrée* and others, and affords them added gaiety.

As the power to rise is proportionate to the strength of the instep, so the step depends on this quality to be done with lightness. To make a *jeté en avant*, suppose that you have the left foot in front and supporting the weight of the body, the right foot [close to it and] ready to move the moment you bend the left knee, and when you rise by straightening the same knee, the force of the extension throws you on the right *demi-pointe* which had passed forwards during the bend. Afterwards you lower the heel to the ground, which completes the *pas*.

Similarly, you may perform several in succession on one foot, repeating them on the other in the same manner, which tends to ease and lightness.

Jetés can be made likewise *en arrière* and *de côté*, that is, by bending on one leg and falling on the *demi-pointe* of the other.

They can also be made in still another manner which

requires more strength in the hop. This is done by rising much quicker, sharply extending the legs, beating one against the other, and falling on the *demi-pointe* of the foot contrary to that on which the bend was made. They then have a different name and are called *demi-cabrioles*.[1] But as this *pas* belongs to theatrical dancing, and since in this treatise I only undertook to give the manner of execution of the *pas* used in ballroom dancing, I shall not trouble the reader to learn this last, which is only suited to those endowed with a particular aptitude for dancing and who make it their profession.

As for ladies, they should not hop so high; it is sufficient for them to keep time by bending, and, as they rise, to come to the ground on the foot contrary to that on which they have bent. Hence, when you dance with a lady and come to *jetés* or other *pas sautés*, you should moderate your hops, to preserve that harmony between the two sexes which is so essential to dancing.

[1] This is similar to a *petit jeté battu en avant*.

CHAPTER XXXVII

Of the Contretemps of the Gavotte, or Contretemps en avant

THE *contretemps* are those *pas sautés* or hopped steps which animate dancing by the variety of ways in which they can be done. Therefore I shall commence with those made *en avant*, which are the easiest.

To make one with the right foot, the body must be supported on the left foot, which is placed in the fourth position, the right foot being back with the heel raised off the ground. Then you bend the left knee, straighten it and rise with a hop, at the same time the right foot passes to the fourth position front and you rise *sur la demi-pointe*, with the legs well extended. Afterwards you make another step forwards in the fourth position with the left foot, which completes the *contretemps*.

It is made similarly *en arrière*. For instance, the left foot being in the fourth position back and supporting the weight of the body, you bend the left knee and at the same time the right leg rises extended and falls behind in the fourth position. Afterwards you make another step backwards with the left foot and *sur la demi-pointe*, but at this last step you lower the heel to the ground, which restores the body to equilibrium and completes the *pas*. This *pas* is made in a bar of light duple time or one of triple time. It takes the same time as a common *pas de bourrée*.

CHAPTER XXXVIII

Of the Different Kinds of Contretemps de côté

THE *contretemps de côté* is made dfferently from that *en avant*, particularly that with the legs crossed; the difference is that while in the former you bend on one foot, in the latter you bend on both. For instance, if you wish to perform a *contretemps* going to the left side, it is done with the right foot. Having both feet in the second position and the body upright, you bend, as shown in Fig. 38, and rise with a hop.

But as the movement made preparatory to hopping is here stronger than that used for rising in a *demi-coupé*, in rising again the right leg throws the weight of the body upon the left, and remains extended sideways off the ground, as shown in Fig. 39, afterwards you make a step with the same foot, crossing it in the fifth position [back], resting the weight of the body on it. Then you make another step sideways in the second position with the left foot, which completes the *pas*.

Many persons make this the same way as that *en avant*, that is, the weight of the body being on the left foot, they bend on it, the right foot being off the ground. But, in my opinion, the body is not so firm; moreover, the right foot moves too quickly and the effect is not so graceful, as

Fig. 38.   First Movement in a Contretemps

Fig. 39. Second Posture after the Hop

I have often observed. For this reason I have given this figure, that it may be more easily understood.

The same *contretemps* are also made *en tournant* and in the same manner; therefore, in executing this *pas* you can make a half-turn or three-quarter turn according to the arrangement of the dance.

It is made in still another manner which is called *contretemps de chaconne* or open *contretemps*, which is different. It is made almost like that *en avant*. That is, the left foot being in front and supporting the weight of the body, the right leg meets it from behind, and you bend the left knee and rise on the left foot with a hop. The right foot, which is off the ground, moves to the second position and the left to the fifth position, front or back, which is the end of the *pas*. Because this *pas* is generally used to move sideways, and is composed of a *mouvement sauté* or movement with a hop, and two *pas marchés sur la demi-pointe*, but at the last the heel must be lowered to the ground so that the body is firm, ready to make whatever step follows. But this manner of making the *pas* is to go to the right, whereas to go to the left the hop must be made on the right foot.

Take care also when bending and hopping to come to the ground in the same place, especially in Ball-room dances, when the steps should be executed with every regard for uniformity and proportion.

There is yet another kind of *contretemps* termed *contretemps à deux mouvements*, also *contretemps ballonné*. This is most graceful and lively, especially for those naturally light-footed, and even confers this quality on those not endowed with it, provided they practise assiduously. To make its manner of execution clear, I shall explain all its varieties.

This *pas* is made *en avant*, *en arrière*, and *de côté*, all performed alike; but I shall begin with that *en avant*. To make it with the right foot, having the left in the fourth position front and supporting the weight of the body, you bend the knee of the latter foot, straighten it and rise with a hop, the right foot which is behind passes forwards as you bend, and remains off the ground during the first movement. Afterwards a second movement is made by bending on the left foot, which throws the body on to the right with a *jeté*. Thus this *pas* is composed of two different movements, that is: a bend and hop on one foot, then a bend on the same foot and a throwing of the body on to the other.[1]

I have said already that all these different *pas* are the same for ladies as for gentlemen, save that the former should not hop so high. But in regard to the bends these should always be well marked, especially when learning them, because they make a dance more pleasing; whereas, if they be not marked, the steps can hardly be distinguished and the dance appears lifeless and dull.

I have said that this *pas* is the same *en arrière*, for the same rules must be observed. That is: you bend and hop on the rear foot, at the same time the front one rises and remains off the ground during the first movement, to be passed backwards when the second movement—a *demi-jeté*—is made, which completes the *pas*.

Those made *de côté* are generally executed after a *pas de bourrée dessus et dessous*, hence you bend and hop on the foot that ends the *pas de bourrée* and that which is in front rises; and at the second movement you come to the ground on that foot, placing it in the second position.

[1] This almost corresponds to a *temps levé* followed by a *jeté*.

CHAPTER XXXIX

Of Chassés of Different Kinds.

SINCE there are several different kinds of *chassés* I shall begin with the easiest, or those which in my opinion are most used in ballroom dances, such as *La Mariée*[1], *l'Allemande*[2], *La Babette* and many others.

This *pas* is generally preceded by a *coupé*, or some other

[1] See Pecour (L.) *Recueil de Dances*, 1700, p. 12, for a stenochoregraphic notation of this dance.
[2] See Rameau, *op. cit.*, Part II., p. 58, for a stenochoregraphic notation of this dance.

step that leads to the second position, because it is begun from this position and made *de côté*, to right or left; but, to explain it more clearly, I shall deal with one side. For instance, if you wish to go to the left, you bend both knees and rise with a hop just off the ground. And in making this movement on both feet, the right approaches the left to fall in its place, so that it forces the latter to move to the second position, which is done very quickly. Because you come to the ground first on the right foot, and the left is placed quickly in the second position, which makes it appear as if one came to the ground on both feet, as it is usual to make two of these steps in succession. For this reason, at the first hop you come to the ground, bend and spring again, transferring the weight of the body to the right or left foot as the next *pas* requires.

But when you have made several in succession, as in the *Allemande*, you make your hops consecutively without rising on one foot, and without rising as in practising, when there are only two as I have just told you.

This *pas* is flowing, because in hopping you gain ground to perform the figure required by the dance. It has a gay effect when several are made in succession, for the dancer appears to be always off the ground, and with but a half spring.

It is done similarly *en arrière*, the positions only being changed. That is, being in the fourth position, right foot front, you bend and rise with a hop backwards, and the right foot, coming to the ground, meets the left in its place and drives it to the fourth position back. But, as you come to the ground with a bent knee, after the second hop you rise, either on the right or the left foot, according to the step that follows; observing always that at the first hop it is the front leg that drives the other, and is always the first to be placed on the ground, as I have said in regard to those made *de côté*.

There is still another kind made *de côté*, like those placed in the fifth strain of *L'Aimable Vainqueur*, in which three made in succession fill a bar of triple time in which the music is composed. But this type of *pas* is more properly a *jeté-chassé*, as will be seen from its manner of execution.

The body being supported on the left foot, you bend on it, and the right, which is off the ground, passes forwards and is extended, and, when you have risen, it crosses with a *jeté* in the third position, which forms this *jeté chassé*. The right foot falling in front of the left takes its place and consequently forces it to rise behind, and the right knee to bend afterwards. But in rising you throw the weight of the body on the left foot, which falls behind in the third position, driving the right and making it rise. Then you bend on the left foot and throw the weight of the body on the right, as in the first step. These three movements must be done in succession without a pause, like the swinging of a pendulum. For the moment you bend on one foot, its movement raises the other, and in rising you throw the weight of the body on the right foot in front, and at the second movement you fall again on the left, whence you comprehend the equilibrium that must be attained in this *pas* if it is to be executed to perfection.

There is yet another manner which closely resembles the last, but differs from it in that it contains two steps. The first is a *jeté* and the second a *pas marché*. It is done as follows: for instance, if you return to the left, having the weight of the body supported on the left foot and the right foot off the ground as shown in Fig. 40, from this position you bend lightly and, as you rise, you bring the right foot to the left, making a *jeté chassé*, allowing the right foot to fall in the third position back, or fifth position back. This movement, owing to the weight of the body, which falls on one foot, raises the left foot, which is afterwards carried sideways, making a *pas marché sur la demi-pointe*. But no sooner is it placed on the ground than the weight of the body is transferred to it, which raises the right foot, and the left heel is lowered to the ground so that it is firm and ready to make another, because these *pas* must be executed very lightly, being but half-movements of the instep, knee and hip. This *pas* has two different *temps*, the right foot being raised at the beginning as shown in Fig. 40. And, in falling on the right foot, the left rises extended as shown in Fig. 41, and from thence

Fig. 40. First Posture of the Chasse in La Babette

Fig 41. Second Posture of the Chassé in La Babette

you move the left to the second position, which completes the *pas*.

They should be done in succession and very lightly, because there are two of them in a bar of light duple time. These kinds of *chassés* afford much gaiety to a dance.

There are still other kinds, but, as I have not encountered them in any ballroom dance, there is no need for me to mention them.

CHAPTER XL

Of Saillies[1] *or Pas Echappés.*

THIS *pas* having appeared to me singular of its kind, and, as it is used in a ballroom dance called *La Babette*, I feel constrained to describe its manner of execution according to the rules.

It seems to me to resemble the *pas tombé*, because a person must be raised *sur les demi-pointes* in order to begin it.

Having risen *sur les demi-pointes*, as I have just said, the feet being in the fourth position and the weight of the body supported equally on both, and supposing the right foot to be in front, from thence you let both feet slip as if your strength failed you, allowing the right to slip backwards and the left forwards, separating them simultaneously. And, in falling, the knees bend and you rise again immediately, placing the right foot in front and the left back, which brings you to your original position. But your knees are still bent and you rise, at the same time throwing the weight of the body on the left foot, and by this *mouvement sauté* you bring the right foot to the left in the first position. Then you make a step with the left foot which is termed *dégager le piéd*,[2] and thus you are free to perform whatever steps follow. But this *enchaînement* is accomplished in two bars of quick duple time and I have

[1] Literally *starts*. [2] A *dégagé*.

endeavoured to describe it in full to make it easy of execution.

This *pas* is also made *en tournant*. They can also be done in this manner. That is, the feet being in the first position and having risen *sur les demi-pointes*, you bend, allowing the feet to slip to the second position, the knees bent in falling; and, in rising, you bring the feet to the first position again, and afterwards *dégager* one or the other ready to make whatever *pas* you wish.

But, to make this description easier to understand, I have set three plates together (see Figs. 42, 43, 44) to show the different *temps*. The first is when you are raised *sur les demi-pointes* with the right foot in front (see Fig. 42). Then you let the two feet slip apart and the right foot, which was in front, falls behind with knee bent. The second figure shows the change at the second movement (see Fig. 43). Then the right foot returns in front with the knees bent as before (see Fig. 42). And the third figure represents the last movement, which ends with an *assemblé* and completes the whole *pas* (see Fig. 44).

CHAPTER XLI

Of the Ouverture de Jambe

THE *Ouverture de Jambe*[1] is a movement which the leg performs to show the agility necessary to keep the body in its equilibrium while the dancer stands on the other leg, and also to demonstrate that he knows how to move it with ease and grace, without which the body loses its balance. It is one of the perfections of dancing to know how to move the legs in making different *pas* and to maintain the upper half of the body in a pleasing position. Besides, this *temps* is made very slowly after a *pas* which has been executed quickly. This affords a variety that denotes a good taste in dancing by investing the slow *pas* with gravity and the quick one with lightness.

[1] Literally *Opening of the Leg.*

Fig. 42. First Posture in the Saillie or Echappé

Fig. 43. Second Posture in the Saillie or Echappé

Fig 44. Third Posture in the Saillie or Echappé

Hence, if you wish to make an *ouverture de jambe* with the left foot, the body must be supported on the right in the fourth position front, that the rear foot may rise from its position and move slowly by the side of the right, crossing in front of it in the form of a semi-circle which ends at the side, the foot remaining off the ground to make whatever other *pas* may be required by the dance. But to give you a clearer demonstration, I shall say that when the left foot moves forwards to cross in front, it extends in approaching the right, and, when it crosses, the knee bends and extends again as it completes the semi-circle, as shown in Fig. 45, where the words: *The half-circle made by the leg* are written.

I have already said in many places that when a *pas* is made with one foot, it should be practised with each foot alternately, which tends to make the perfect dancer and gives him the facility of learning quicker. Moreover, owing to this regular exercise, the body is carried with an ease which it maintains in all the various movements which dancing requires, and with that grace and precision which this art alone can procure.

CHAPTER XLII

Of Battements of Different Kinds.

BATTEMENTS are also movements off the ground made by one foot while the body is supported on the other, and make dancing very brilliant, particularly when made easily, and, as they are executed in several ways and introduced into many ballroom dances, I shall give the manner of making them.

First, you must know that the hip and knee form and govern this movement, the hip guiding the thigh in opening or closing, while the knee, by its flexion, makes the *battement* by crossing in front of, or behind, the supporting leg.

Suppose, then, that you are standing on the left foot,

Fig. 45.   Demonstration of the Ouverture de Jambe

with the right off the ground and well extended. You cross it in front of the left by bringing the thigh close to the supporting leg and bending the knee, and extend it by opening it sideways, and bend the knee again to cross it behind. Then you extend it sideways again and make several in succession with either foot. This renders the legs supple and enables you to execute these *pas* quickly; but take care to straighten the knee after you have bent it.

These *pas* are very useful in dancing, and are combined with others to afford them variety and add to the enjoyment of the dance.

They are sometimes done while hopping, as in the example in the third strain of the *Allemande*. This *pas* begins with a kind of *contretemps*, by hopping on one foot, afterwards the foot that is off the ground makes two *battements*, one *devant*, one *derrière*, and opens to the fourth position back, when the weight of the body is transferred to it, so that the *pas* may be repeated with the other foot. In making this *pas*, the body should be shaded on the same side as the working foot; that is, if the *battement* be made with the right foot, the right shoulder should be drawn backwards.

Sometimes, simple *battements* are combined with other *pas*. For instance, you make a *coupé en avant* with the left foot, and the right foot which is behind makes a *battement* by striking the left leg, then opens to the fourth position back. But the *battement* is made with the knees straight, because, in the *demi-coupés en avant*, you should rise *sur la demi-pointe* with the knees straight, and it is then that you execute this *battement*, the right foot passing *en arrière*, when the left heel should be lowered to the ground, which makes it easy for the right foot to pass to the fourth position, as I have already explained in the chapter on *coupés*.

There are other *battements*, made differently from these, in which the hips only take part, as in *entrechats*, *cabrioles*, and other *pas de ballet*, which would require too much space to describe. Therefore, I shall bring this first part to an end in order to begin the second; which teaches the carriage of the arms proper to each *pas*.

Part Two.

CHAPTER I

A Discourse on the Arms and of the Importance of Knowing how to Move them Gracefully.

NOTHING is more advantageous to those who have an aptitude for dancing and a disposition to dance well, than to apply themselves to the study of the proper carriage of the arms. For this reason, they should read with the greatest attention the rules I am about to lay down, that they will more easily understand their lessons and make progress.

Indeed, a good master knows how to place his pupil's arms in accordance with his physical formation. To make him hold them higher if he be of short stature, to lower them to the level of the hips if he be tall. But, if the pupil be of medium height, he should hold them in a line with the pit of the stomach—a remark I have known to be uttered by one of the most skilful masters of our time.

Moreover, everyone knows that M. Beauchamps was one of the first to introduce and lay down rules, and from thence has arisen the desire common to so many persons of both sexes to practise them to increase all the graces they have to-day, which they would not possess but for the care and attention bestowed upon them.

For my part, I shall only say that I regard the arms which adorn the body, as a frame made for a picture. But, if it do not harmonise with the picture, however beautiful it may be, its value is less.

Hence, however well a dancer may perform his steps, if

he have not soft and graceful arms his dance will appear lifeless, and consequently will have the same effect as a picture without a frame.

Some persons assert that it is a particular gift. I agree. Nevertheless, I hope that I shall not fail to give the precepts for its acquisition by a full and complete demonstration in this part, which should contribute no less to the improvement of youth than to the help of their masters, which is the sole aim of my book.

CHAPTER II

Of the Position of the Arms and their correct Elevation.

SINCE the beauty of the body in dancing depends, as I have already said, on knowing how to dispose the arms gracefully, it is impossible to devote too much care to their position, so that they can move with the necessary freedom.

Therefore, I assume that a person should be well proportioned and of medium height, whence, in my opinion and in accordance with the rules, the arms should be raised in a line with the pit of the stomach, as shown in Fig. 46. The dancer is represented full face, so that all the parts may be seen in their true proportions. The head is erect, the weight of the body supported equally on both legs, with the feet in the second position, which is relative to the arms. For, the legs being open and the two feet placed on the same line, the arms should be likewise open and raised equally. Because if they were higher, they would resemble a cross; moreover, they would tend to be stiff and not possess the same grace.

Nevertheless, as no rule is without an exception and since one is obliged to soften or conceal natural faults, it is the master's duty to adapt the rules to his pupils' requirements. For instance, if a person be of short stature, he must raise the arms a little higher to add to his height,

Fig. 46. The Elevation of the Arms for Dancing

which consequently affords him more grace. Similarly, if the pupil be tall, he should not raise his arms higher than the hip, which thus remedies in some degree this disproportion and affords a grace which, without this care, would be lacking.

I have shown the hands neither open nor closed, so that the movements of the wrist and elbow may be made with all that grace and freedom which should be observed in these movements. On the other hand, if the thumb be pressed against one of the fingers, this will stiffen the other joints and detract from that ease.

I am not greatly taken with the posture I have given to my figures for the elevation of the arms. I have, however, submitted them to the criticism of the most skilful persons both in dancing and drawing, and, in their opinion, they are drawn correctly according to rule, both in their relation to the body and to be able to move with ease in the different *pas*, wherein must be observed that opposition which is the adornment of dancing.

CHAPTER III

Of the Different Movements of the Arms.

THERE are three different movements of the arms as for the legs, which are related one to the other: those of the wrists, elbows, and shoulders. But they must harmonise with those of the legs, so that if you make *demi-coupés* in *temps* and *ouvertures de jambe*, and other *pas* which are taken more from the instep than the knee, it is the wrist that should move. Whereas, in the case of *pas* where the bending is greater, as in *pas de bourrée, temps de courante, pas de sissonne, contretemps* and others which require contrast or opposition, then it is the elbow that moves, or which is most in evidence, because the elbow must not be bent unless the movement is accompanied with that of the wrist. It is the same with the instep and knee, which cannot complete its movement unless one rises on the *demi-pointe*, which is achieved by the instep.

As for the movement of the shoulder, it is not apparent except in the *pas tombé* where, owing to the inclination of the body, it seems as if one lacked strength. Thus the shoulder by its movement does as if the arms fell, as will be explained hereafter in the manner of moving the arms to each *pas*.

These movements of the shoulder again appear in opposition in that the arms being extended, the shoulder is drawn backwards; for instance, if you go to the side of a person, you shade the shoulder.

But, to give a clearer notion of it, I shall explain in the following chapters the manner of moving the wrists separately from that of the elbows, so that you will know the difference and can attain that graceful precision which dancing demands.

CHAPTER IV

Of the Manner of Moving the Wrist.

ALTHOUGH the movements of the wrist do not appear difficult, they merit proper attention, for infinite graces reside in these extremities, when the arms are moved smoothly according to the rules I shall describe. That is why I shall give figures wherever necessary to make my instructions easy of interpretation.

This will be observed in Fig. 47, where (1) represents the hand turned upwards, and (2) the hand turned downwards; that is, one is the contrary of the other.

But as the movement of the wrist is done in two ways, *viz.*, from above downwards, and from below upwards, therefore, when the movement is done in the first manner, the wrist must be bent inwards making a turn of the hand, which, from this same movement, returns to the first position as shown in (3) by the words : *The turn of the wrist,*

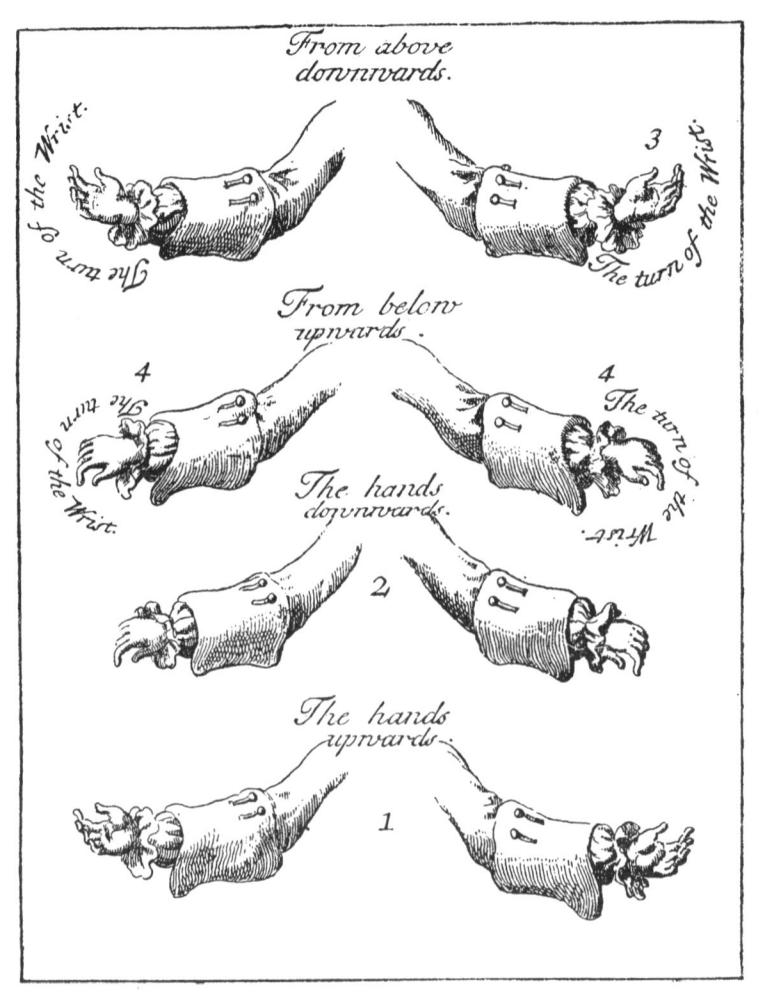

Fig. 47. First Representation of the Arms showing the Movement of the Wrists

which demonstrates the manner according to the first representation of the arms (2). But care must be taken not to bend the wrist too much, which would make it appear broken.

As for the second movement, which is made from below upwards, the hands being downwards as shown in (2), bend the wrist as in (4), then let the hand return upwards, making a semi-circle according to the words: *The turn of the wrist*, and by this movement the hands are in the position as in (1).

CHAPTER V

Of the Movement of the Elbow and Shoulder.

THE elbow, like the wrist, has its movement from above downwards, and from below upwards; with this difference, that when you bend the elbows the wrists move too, which prevents the arms from being stiff and accords them considerable grace. Nevertheless, the bend of the wrist must not be exaggerated, for that would appear extravagant. The same observations apply to the feet, for when you bend the knee it is the instep that completes the movement by rising on the step, and so of the elbow with the wrist.

But as these movements demand a full understanding and since the explanatory figures which I have employed throughout the book seem to me as necessary as the discourse, I feel obliged to repeat the former plate that nothing may be wanting to ensure the correct execution of these movements.

Therefore, to move the arms from above downwards, the arms being placed as shown in Fig. 48 (5), the elbow and wrist must be bent according to the words: *The turn of the elbow, The turn of the wrist*. And when the wrists are bent (6), you extend them (8), and the arms return to their original position (5). Thus, when you make a movement

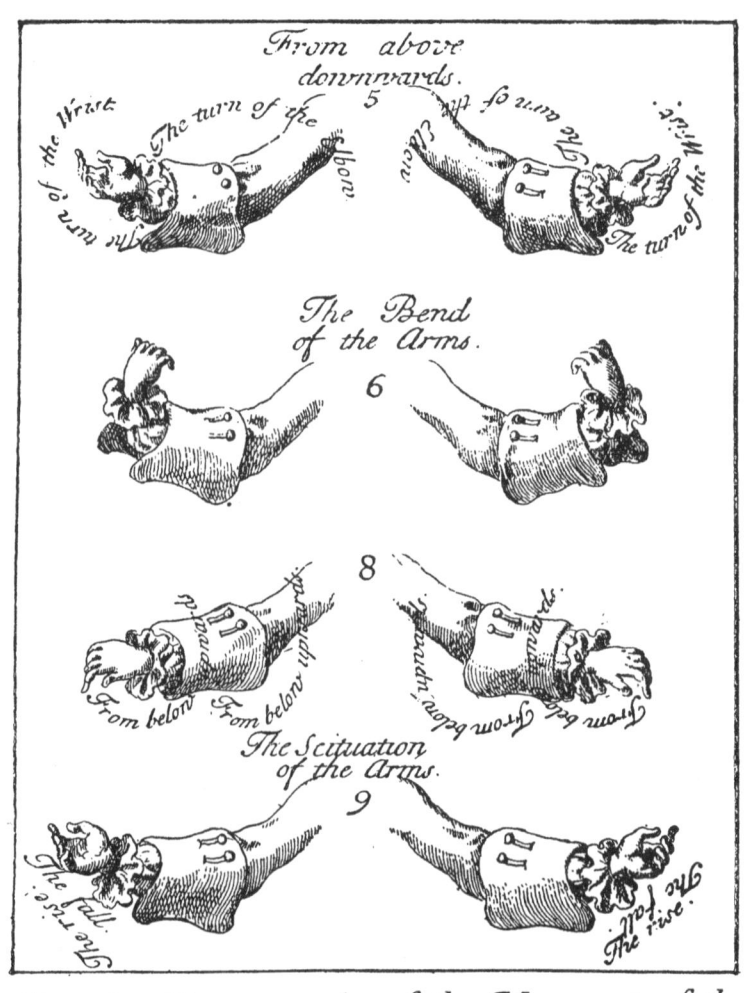

Fig. 48.   Representation of the Movements of the Wrists, Elbows and Shoulders

of the wrists, they should bend and extend as if they were bent with the elbows.

As for the second movement, which is made from below upwards, the hands are turned downwards as shown (8), the wrists and elbows being bent in making a circle only, according to the words: *From below upwards*, to show that both arms ought to bend together equally and return to the original position (5).

This last movement from below upwards is as necessary as the first, because there are *pas* in which the arms must be moved upwards by opposition; for, generally, the extended arm is turned downwards and bends in opposition to the contrary foot, which is explained at length in the next chapter.

In regard to the movement of the shoulders, as they are scarcely observed, except in *pas tombés*, where the arms are extended (9), they must fall a little lower than the hips, without bending either elbows or wrists, as shown by the words: *The fall, The rise*, by each arm; for, when they fall, they rise to the height occupied before they were turned, which is achieved solely by a movement of the shoulders.

CHAPTER VI

Of the Opposition of the Arms to the Feet.

OF all the movements made in dancing, the opposition or contrast of the arm to the leg is the most natural and requires the least attention. For instance, if you look at different persons walking, you will observe that when they step forwards with the right foot, the left arm will naturally oppose it, which seems to be a definite rule.

Skilful dancers have moved their arms according to this rule, bringing the arm in opposition to the foot; that is, when the right foot is in front, the left arm should be in opposition for the whole extent of the step. I say the extent of the step, because in the *temps de courante*, which is but one step, if it be made with the right foot, the left arm is in opposition to it. Similarly, in the *pas de bourrée* or *fleuret en avant*, which, although it consists of three steps, does not require three changes of the arms, it is sufficient if they be opposed at the first step.

But, as this opposition requires a fuller explanation, I have drawn this figure (see Fig. 49), to show the proper positions. The body is upright, the head turned towards the opposite arm, which is the right and bent in front of you. The hand is in a line with the shoulder and a little forwards. The left arm is extended sideways and drawn a little backwards, but in a line with the pit of the stomach. The body is supported on the left foot, with the right heel off the ground ready to make a step.

But, when you desire to change the opposition, take care that your arms move together and that each makes a contrary movement, so that the arm which is extended turns downwards (3), and that which is opposite (2), describes a semi-circle according to the words: *The turn of the elbow from above downwards*, which should be done at the same time, one with the other, so that both may simultaneously be turned downwards as shown (4).

Both arms being down, the left arm returned *from below upwards* (5), according to the words: *The turn of the elbow from below upwards*, the right only turns the hand upwards, which is done by a little turn of the wrist *from below upwards*, which completes the change of opposition as shown in (6) and (7).

Although I have stated that these movements should be made together, I again repeat that they should be performed smoothly and in succession. And that the execution may be easier, I would advise you to practise in front of a mirror, moving your arms in the manner I have laid down, when, if you be possessed of a modicum of discernment and good taste, the mirror will reveal your faults, which consequently you will be able to correct.

These are the shortest and quickest methods I can give you for making your arm movements with that grace and precision the art requires.

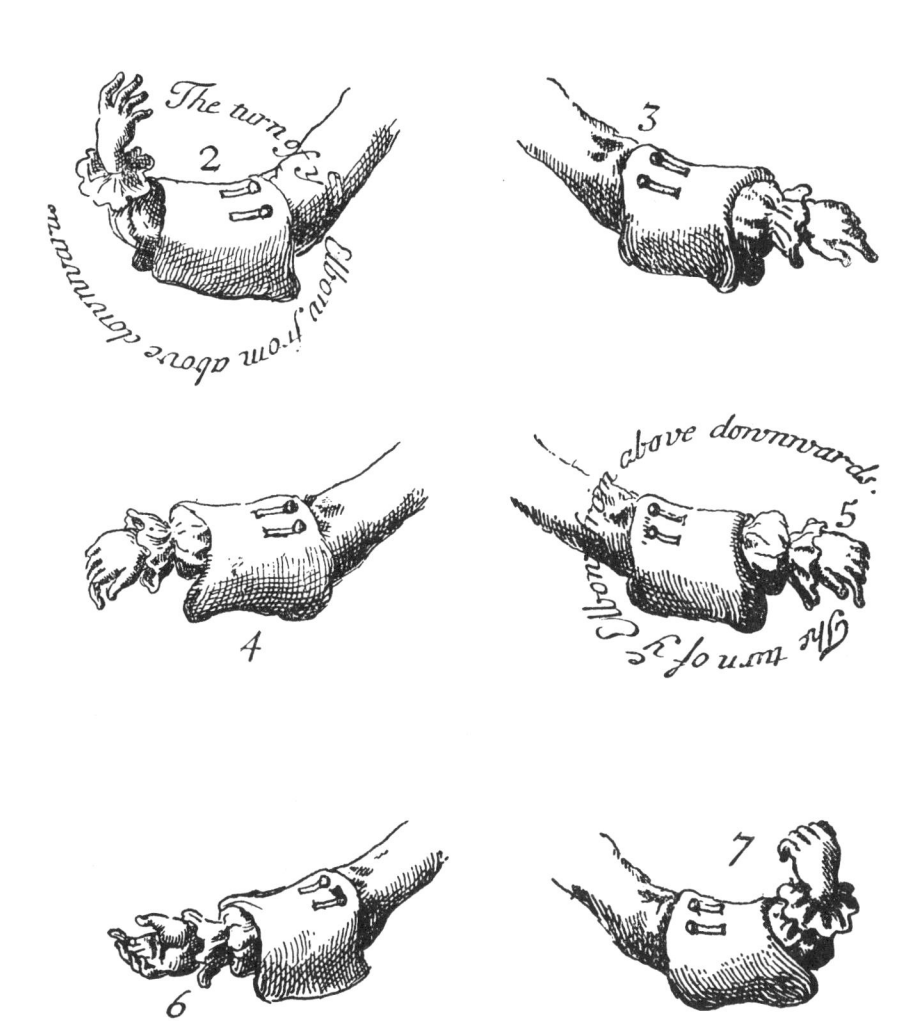

Fig. 49. Demonstration of the Change of Opposition

NOTE.—The words to No. 5 should read: *The turn of the elbow from below upwards.*

CHAPTER VII

Of the Manner of Moving the Arms in the Temps de Courante and Demi-Coupés en arrière.

WHEN a person has acquired a facility to move his arms with the requisite grace and desires to combine such actions with the movements of his feet, he can choose no easier *pas* than the *temps de courante* or *pas grave*, which is a very slow movement. Thus he will learn to move his arms and legs in harmony, and for this reason I have placed these four figures in succession to explain the different positions to be taken by the arms and legs.

First, you must remember the manner of execution of the *temps de courante*, which is to bend and rise before passing the foot forwards.

In the first plate (see Fig. 50), the body is supported on the right foot in the fourth position front (1), the left heel off the ground, the toe touching the ground and consequently ready to make a step, the left arm opposite the right foot, and the right arm (5) extended, the hand outwards (6); and the writing forming a semi-circle (7) is to show the path the [left] arm is to take.

To begin the *pas* the left foot must be brought up to the right, during which the left elbow is to be turned as shown by the words: *The turn of the elbow from above downwards*, which forms the semi-circle, and you trace the turn which the arm makes *from above downwards*, as the other words: *The turn of the wrist*, show the movement of the right wrist.

Fig. 51 shows how far you should bend. The body is supported on the right foot (2), the left off the ground (3), the two heels one against the other, and the arms, palms of the hands downwards, at the same height (4). To perform these movements with ease, these figures should be studied in every detail, thence you will acquire a proper knowledge of the movements of the arms and legs.

Fig. 52 shows how to rise after the bend (which may be termed in equilibrium). The body is supported on the

*Fig. 50.   Preparatory Position for the Execution
of the Temps de Courante*

Fig. 51. Second Posture in the Temps de Courante

Fig. 52.   The Movement of the Instep in the
             Temps de Courante

right *demi-pointe* (3), the left leg extended like the right, but with the foot off the ground (4), the palms of the hands half-turned upwards (5).

Fig. 53 is intended to show the opposition to the left foot making a step forwards, so that as you glide it to the fourth position front, the right arm forms its contrast. Thus the step and movement of the arms end together.

But as one cannot devote too much care to the proper carriage of the arms in dancing, and since all depends on a good beginning, I pray you glance at Fig. 53, in which the right arm (6) is in opposition to the left foot (7), which is in front; and the left arm (8) is extended and drawn backwards, likewise the shoulder, which makes the opposition correct according to the rules of the art.

Though I have given a full description of these four different plates, it is only for your better understanding, that you may comprehend the different movements. But when you come to put them into practice, you must understand that they are to explain but one *pas*, and that the different movements succeed one another without any pause.

But, to learn to practise them equally well with either foot, I should advise you to begin at the bottom of the room.

I have explained this so clearly, in order that you may do them one after the other with either foot and continue them several times until you have reached the top. Then you will do the *demi-coupés en arrière*, observing, after you have finished your last step, to lower the rear foot to the ground and support the body thereon, so as to make them in the following manner.

Supposing your last step to be made with the right foot, the left arm will be in front, in opposition to it. Therefore you bend the left leg (according to the manner of executing *demi-coupés*) and, as you bend, the opposite arm makes its semi-circle *from above downwards*, and the arm which was extended returns *from below upwards*, which makes your opposition.

Observe also that, in going backwards, it is the same arm and foot which move, because that always makes the opposition. For instance, if the *demi-coupé* be made with

Fig. 53. Commencement of the Opposition

the right foot, the right arm moves forwards *from below upwards*.

There are many different *temps* included in the *temps de courante*. You even have *pas graves* made *de côté*; but these *temps* are open, in that they are usually made from the third position to the second, which is an open position, and consequently requires no opposition; the arms being open in this *temps*, a slight movement must be made with both arms, and also with the wrists *from below upwards*.

For instance, the arms being open and the hands turned as shown in Fig. 52, in bending they must be turned downwards, and in rising and completing the *temps*, there should be made a little movement of the elbow and wrist *from below upwards*, which restores them to their original position.

CHAPTER VIII

Of the Manner of Moving the Arms with Pas de Bourrée or Fleurets.

HAVING made every endeavour to afford you a clear explanation of the different movements of the arms, with the rules governing the actions of the wrist, elbow and shoulder, and at the same time made you aware of the opposition or contrast of the leg to the arm, I have only now to show you how to make them appropriate to each *pas*, by instructing you simply in the oppositions or contrasts you should observe, without repeating the manner in which they should be done, which, in my opinion, has been fully dealt with already.

I shall say then that if you make a *pas de bourrée en avant* with the right foot, the change of the arms should be made thus: the right arm, which is in opposition to the left foot, should be extended as you bend the knee, while the left arm turns downwards at the same time to bend in front of you; the right foot moves forwards for the body to rise upon it, which makes the opposition of the left arm to the right leg. As to the two steps which follow and complete your *pas de bourrée*, you must not change your arms since there is but one opposition in this *pas*.

For *pas de bourrée en arrière* the same rule applies as in the case of *demi-coupés*. That is to say, if your *pas de bourrée* be made with the right foot, in making your *demi-coupé en arrière* with the same foot, the right arm should bend, as the opposition is only seen from the front. Therefore, as a general rule, when a step backwards is made with one foot, the arm of the same side makes the opposition.

As regards the *pas de bourrée dessus et dessous*, if you make it with the right foot going to the left, in crossing your right foot the left arm makes the opposition and the right is extended. But at the second step of your *pas de bourrée*, which is made with the left foot, and which you carry sideways to the second position, the left arm opens; and, as you draw the right foot to the third position back, which makes the third movement of your *pas de bourrée*, the right arm bends in opposition to the left foot, which is in front. This produces two oppositions in this *pas*, but sometimes they are not made because of the *enchaînement* of another *pas* which follows, and alters the rule; for it may happen that you may be obliged to bend both arms to make this next step; but your master will instruct you accordingly.

When these *pas* are made *en tournant*, observe the rules laid down above.

As to the *pas de bourrée emboîté*, two oppositions are necessary; one as you begin to make your *demi-coupé*, and the other at the last step you make. For instance, you commence your *pas* with the right foot, and you carry it to the fourth position back, which obliges you to bend the right arm to make the opposition to the left foot in front.

But no sooner are you raised on the right foot, than the left passes to the third position back, and you wait a little *sur les demi-pointes*, the legs extended, without changing your arms; and when you slide the right foot forwards, which is the last step of your *pas de bourrée*, the right arm extends backwards, shading the shoulder, and the left bends in front, making its contrast with the right foot.

There is another kind of *pas de bourrée* made *sur place* and to the presence; but as this *pas* is open at the beginning, the arms follow the step. For instance, you make your *demi-coupé* with the right foot sideways in the second position, and, as both your arms are open, you bend both wrists, making a whole turn *from above downwards*. I call it a whole turn because the hands return to their original position; but at the second step, which you make sideways (as described in the manner of its execution), in drawing the other foot behind, which makes the third step, you bend the same arm as the foot you draw behind, which makes the contrast with the front foot.

The manner of moving the arms in this *pas* differs from that in the others, because you oppose the arm to the foot at the beginning, whereas in this case you only make the opposition at the last step.

It is also performed in yet another manner sideways, shading the shoulder, of which kind of *pas* there are two in the first strain of *L'Aimable Vainqueur*, in *La Bretagne*[1], in *La Nouvelle Forlanne*[1] and many others, in which the opposition is only made at the end of the *pas*. For instance, suppose you have the left foot in front and the right arm opposed, you make a *demi-coupé* by bending on the left foot and rising on the right, at the same time extending the arm, which enables you to shade the body or turn sideways a little, and the left foot being carried behind, you stay *sur les demi-pointes*. Then you slide the right foot to the fourth position front, the left arm bending at the same time and also moving forwards in opposition to the right foot.

There are also others called *pas de bourrée vites*,[2] or *pas de bourrée à deux mouvements*,[3] which are made *en avant* and *de côté*. As to the arms, there is but one opposition; in that if the step be done with the right foot, the left arm bends in front, and when you make the last step of this *pas de bourrée*, which is a *demi-jeté*, the left arm is extended; thus both arms are open.

[1] See Rameau, *op. cit.*, Part II, pp. 65 and 72, for stenochoregraphic notations of these dances.
[2] Quick *pas de bourrée*.
[3] *Pas de bourrée* of two movements.

But when you make this *pas* sideways, it is slightly different, in that if you make your *demi-coupé* with the right foot, crossing it in front of the left, the left arm comes into opposition, to be extended during the second and third steps; and when you draw the right foot behind, in falling on the left for a fourth step (which is a kind of *pas tombé*), then both the extended arms are slightly lowered and raised again; which completes the movement of the arms in this *pas*.

CHAPTER IX

Of the Manner of Moving the Arms with different kinds of Coupés

AS the movements of the arms to be used with the various kinds of *coupés* vary according to the *enchaînement* of which the dance is composed, I shall describe several varieties for your guidance, beginning with those made *en avant*.

Supposing you wish to execute a *coupé en avant* with the right foot, you should have the left foot in front and the right arm opposed; then, in bending for your *demi-coupé*, you extend that arm, turning it *from below upwards*, without bending the left; but when you slide the left foot forwards, which is the second part of your *coupé*, the right arm bends in front, and makes a proper contrast of the arm to the foot.

There are others in which the foot is opened sideways *sur la demi-pointe*, without transferring the weight of the body thereon; for, having then extended one arm in your *demi-coupé*, you leave them both open as shown in Fig. 46, which demonstrates the correct elevation of the arms; for when you are in the second position, there is no contrast, unless the *pas* be followed by a *pas en tournant*, which is very rare, since turns should be begun from the first or fourth position.

Others end with an *ouverture de jambe*, when you should

observe the same rule as for *demi-coupés*, which is to extend the same arm as the foot with which the *pas* is made; yet neither arm is to make any movement during the *ouverture de jambe*.

There are still others made *en avant*, that is, having extended the arm during the execution of the *demi-coupé*, you move it with the same foot, if you are to turn, because this arm should act as a guide or counterpoise for you to turn; therefore, as a general rule, if you turn to the right, you bend the right arm, because it afterwards extends, and by its motion affords the body ease in turning; the same rule applies when you turn to the left.

The *coupé en arrière* is different in that it requires two oppositions. One in bending for your *demi-coupé*; supposing it to be made with the right foot, the right arm makes the opposition and returns at the same time. The other opposition occurs when the left foot steps backwards, when the left arm returns in front, and is in opposition to the other foot.

For those made *de côté*, if you begin them with the right foot, you make an opposition with the left arm in making your *demi-coupé*, extending the arm during the second step, which is open; hence there is no opposition.

In my opinion, I think a movement of both wrists can be made in this *coupé*, which seems to be simpler.

There are some made *en avant* and concluded *en arrière*, the manner of which is unusual in that if you make a *demi-coupé en avant* with the right foot, in rising, the left is brought up to the right, making a beat behind, and returned to its former place, the fourth position back, which makes the *coupé* complete in this *pas* by making the *demi-coupé en avant* with the right foot, where the left arm is brought into opposition with it; and, to distinguish it better, the right shoulder is shaded, and its arm drawn well backwards, which makes the body free and graceful. For those made *en avant*, and with a beat at the second step, no movement of the arms should be made during the beat; because this *pas* is designed merely to show how free your legs can be without disturbing the upper part of your body, which detracts from the grace which should ever be maintained.

CHAPTER X

Of the Manner of Moving the Arms in Coupés of Movement

I HAVE separated these *coupés* of movement from the others to avoid confusion, and to make you sensible of all that grace which they should possess. This *pas* is made *en avant* and *de côté*, but, as I would keep to the same plan throughout, that is, to begin with the easiest manner, I shall commence with those made *en avant*.

Therefore, when you make your first step, which is a *demi-coupé*, well sustained, you simultaneously let both arms turn slightly downwards, and you make a half movement with the wrists and elbows, beginning *from below upwards*, which should be accompanied by a slight, imperceptible and unaffected inclination of the head and body. But, on making your second movement, which is a *jeté échappé*, in beginning your bend, your arms extend and at the same time have a slight movement of the shoulder in falling; while, on rising, the body returns to its former position, likewise the head, which should be held a little backwards. This accords a majestic air and effects a perfect union of the movements of the legs and arms, as well as those of the head and body.

As regards those made *de côté*, although the movements of the arms are made somewhat after the same manner, there are, nevertheless, certain observations to be heeded. For instance, when you execute your *demi-coupé* (supposing it to be done with the right foot), as it crosses in the fifth position front, it obliges you to make use of the rule of opposition: to shade the right shoulder a little and allow the left to come slightly forwards, which consequently produces the opposition to the right foot, without, nevertheless, preventing your making those movements of the arms *from below upwards.* But lower the arms slightly in the execution of your second movement and then raise them in finishing, also make a small inclination of the body and head; and note that, if you go from the right, the head should be half turned in that direction. When all these observations are put into practice, they have a wonderful effect on dancing, and accord it that vivacity and good taste which it would otherwise lack.

CHAPTER XI

Of the Manner of Moving the Arms in the Pas Tombé and Pas de Gaillarde.

SINCE I have already explained, in Part I, the *pas tombé* and *pas de gaillarde*, these being composed of many other steps and movements, permit me to explain the manner of moving the arms according to those different steps. For instance, if it be simply a *pas tombé*, you must, as already described, begin by rising *sur les demi-pointes*, with the arms placed as shown in Fig. 46; therefore, when the foot is drawn behind in falling, the arms, though extended, fall; which is done by the movement of the shoulders, which extend, letting the arms fall and rise immediately. By that means you observe the harmony between the legs and the arms, since while the foot is drawn behind and your knees bend as if their strength failed (in the manner of the *pas tombé*), the arms likewise fall, to rise again when you make your second step, which completes the *pas tombé*, and is a *demi-jeté*. Hence in this *pas* the arms simply fall and rise in accordance with the movement of the shoulders.

In *pas de gaillarde*, the arms must be moved differently, in that they begin with an *assemblé*; therefore the arms are turned downwards before you bend, then you bring them together and the wrists are half bent, turning *from below upwards.* But when you make your second step, which is sideways to the second position, your arms, in returning *from above downwards*, are extended as in the first position. So that, when you rise on the foot with which you stepped sideways, to draw the other behind after it, the arms move as explained in the *pas tombé*; that is, they fall and rise again.

There is also another *pas* made *en avant*, which resembles the *pas de gaillarde*, which I have heard termed *sissonne de chaconne*. In this, since it is made forwards, you oppose an arm to the contrary foot. But, as I have already explained, this *pas* begins with an *assemblé*, therefore, if it be made with the right foot in front, the left arm must move in front *from below upwards* to make the contrast.

For instance, in the execution of the *assemblé*, the right arm, which was in front, extends turning downwards, and at the same time the left does likewise and comes into opposition with the right leg, which is closed in front of the left; but no sooner is this *assemblé* made than the right foot slides into the fourth position, and, in sliding, the body and head make a little movement and recover as you rise on this right foot and the left arm extends. Then both arms remain in that position, without making any movement during the two *jetés chassés* which complete the *pas*.

CHAPTER XII

Of the Manner of Moving the Arms in Pirouettes

ALTHOUGH the *pirouette* is one of those *pas* which are made *sur place* and seems to require little attention, it demands as great a care as any other. This is what makes the art of dancing so extensive, since, in the very *pas* which appear to be the easiest, there exist infinite graces which must be acquired to dance well. For this reason, I exhort all who seek improvement to pay heed to such matters.

This *pas* is generally preceded by another, such as the *coupé*, which is the preparation for that to follow. For instance, the pointing of the toes and the *ouverture de jambe*, which ends with the foot off the ground, are the preparation for making a *pirouette* ; therefore I will show you how to order the arms ; and, that you may the more clearly understand, I have drawn this figure (see Fig. 54), which shows the essential details, by which you may easily comprehend the movements the arms should make.

In this figure, the dancer is shown supported on the right foot (1), the left foot off the ground (2), the right arm extended (3), the left arm bent (4), and the head turned to the left (5).

But when you bend on the right foot and the left crosses at the same time (as I have already said when describing its manner of execution), in rising *sur la demi-pointe*, the arm extends with a turn of the elbow and wrist, as is expressed by the words : *The whole turn of the arm*, which accompanies the body in its turning, making an easy and complete turn of the arm *from below upwards* and returning to the position shown in Fig. 54.

Observe also to hold your head very erect, to preserve the equilibrium of the body, because it should turn on one foot as on a pivot, as I have endeavoured to express in my drawing, by showing the dancer supported perpendicularly on one foot and looking to the left, in order to move with that precision and ease required by the movement.

Some *pirouettes* are executed with a spring, in which the arms move very similarly, except that they imitate the legs a little in their movement by rising more quickly during the spring and extending with more vivacity, which makes it easy for the body to turn on the same side on which the arm extends.

Nevertheless, although these movements are made with a spring, they should be kept under control, for since this *pas* is made by turning, so to speak, *sur place,* if you sprang too high the body would be thrown out of its centre of gravity by the efforts you would be forced to make in order to rise. Besides, social dances being graceful measures in themselves, require easy and polite movements only.

Fig. 54. Preparatory Position for the Execution of a Pirouette

CHAPTER XIII

Of the Manner of Moving the Arms with Balancés

THE *balancé* is one of the easiest of dance steps, and one to which considerable grace may be imparted. It accords with any time, and always produces a good effect; but since there are several ways of performing it, as I have said already, I shall give two ways of moving the arms with it.

Therefore, when you make your first step in the second position—this step being made after another which obliges you to have an arm in opposition to it—the arm which is opposed in front extends *from above downwards*, and the other arm which is extended makes a small movement of the wrist *from above downwards*; because, whenever you make a movement with one arm to maintain the harmony, you must make a small movement with the other that is extended; for it is these little details that give rise to the grace and delicacy which I have already mentioned.

As to the other *balancés* which are made in the fourth position front, if you begin with the right foot, the right arm which is in front extends moving *from above downwards*, and the left arm, turning down, bends in opposition to the right foot in returning *from below upwards*, which is the contrary movement. But at the second *demi-coupé*, the head turns a little to the right, then inclines slightly, and rises again with this step, for, as you rise on the left foot, the head rises also, which makes each in perfect harmony with the other.

CHAPTER XIV

Of the Manner of Moving the Arms in the Pas de Sissonne

HAVING afforded you the easiest explanation of making this *pas*, you have now only to know how to move the arms with the requisite grace, for as this *pas* follows another, so every step has its contrast.

Supposing you have the left foot in front, then the right arm should be in opposition. Hence, in making your first movement, your right arm also makes at the same time its movement *from above downwàrds*. At that instant, the left turns down and bends, in opposition to the right foot which crosses in front of the left, and on which you make a second hop without changing the opposition of the left arm; since this second hop is made on the right foot which is in front, and the arm is in contrast to the foot.

I have also told you that it is made *sur place* after another manner, thus: at the first spring by falling on both feet, and at the second by rising on the rear foot, which needs no alteration in the arms, since the right foot is in front, and the opposition correct.

In the case of *pas de sissonne* made *en tournant*, the opposite arm must be used for the turn—there are many such examples in ballroom dances. For instance, at the end of the first strain of *La Mariée*, where there are *two contretemps de côté* with the right foot; the left arm, which is in opposition, in extending causes you by its movement to make the half turn to the left. But as the right foot crosses behind, the right arm also bends, in contrast with the left foot in front.

As a general rule, in *pas en tournant*, the arm of the side to which you turn gives you impetus, for by its motion it obliges the body to turn on the side towards which it extends.

As regards *pas de sissonne en arrière* the same rule holds as in other *pas en arrière*; *viz*. the same arm and same leg move.

I should advise those who are desirous of moving their arms with ease, to begin by practising these steps with their appropriate arm movements, for as these *pas* afford lightness to the body, so they also endow the arms with a sense of freedom.

CHAPTER XV

Of the Manner of Moving the Arms in Pas de Rigaudon and Jetés

THE arms in the *pas de rigaudon* are the least troublesome, and it is easy to understand the reason, which I shall explain in a few words. This *pas* is made *sur place*, and contains no movements that require a great deal of strength, for, properly speaking, it is merely a play of the instep which forces the other joints to make some movement; therefore, in the arms the wrists only move, that is: once *from below upwards* and then *from above downwards*.

First, when you bend on both feet to raise the right foot, in this movement you bend both wrists *from above downwards*, and extend them on rising. But, when you bend both feet to make your last spring, you likewise bend both wrists, raising them *from below upwards*, which leads to harmony between the legs and arms.

It should be noted that in this *pas* there is a close relation between the wrists and insteps, since they are the only joints that bend.

Jetés, too, are *pas* made by the movement of the instep, therefore it is only the wrists that move. For instance, suppose you make one *jeté* with the right foot and one with the left, so that you make two in succession which are equal to another *pas*, and thus to a bar of duple time. Then, on beginning with the right foot, you make a slight movement only with the wrists *from above downwards*, and the arms remain extended during the second step; but, as these two steps are made in succession, and are slight movements only, therefore the arms should not be moved.

The same observation applies to the arms when you make *jetés en arrière*; above all take heed to make the movements softly, so as not to disturb the upper part of the body, that it may retain that graceful manner it should possess.

CHAPTER XVI

Of the Manner of Moving the Arms in Contretemps of the Gavotte

THIS is one of the principal *pas* used in dancing, both for its antiquity as for the different ways in which it is executed, for it is made sometimes *en avant*, sometimes *en arrière*, also *de côté* and *en tournant*. In short, whatever time be used, it can easily be introduced into the dance, which it animates by its springing motion and variety.

Let us begin with that made *en avant*, as being the easiest, and supposing it to be made with the right foot, the left must be in the fourth position front, therefore the right arm should be in opposition; for then, in bending on the left foot to spring on it, the right arm simultaneously extends in turning *from above downwards* and the left wrist also bends *from above downwards*. But these three movements must be made at the same time; that is to say, when you bend on the left foot, the arms make their movement that instant.

If this *pas* be made *en arrière*, the arms and legs move in the same manner.

But, as regards those made *de côté*, they are executed differently as regards both legs and arms, and since I have demonstrated the steps in Part I, by means of text and explanatory plates, I feel obliged to place three figures here showing the different parts of this *pas* and their corresponding arm movements. Thus, suppose you have both feet in the second position and the body is supported on both feet, as shown in Fig. 55, in which both arms are extended, with the words: *The course of the arms* against each, this is to show from what position the arms should bend.

When the movement of the *contretemps* is taken, the head is erect, the body supported on both feet, the knees bent and the waist steady (see Fig. 56). But in rising with the hop you alight on the left foot, and your arms extend according to the turn expressed by the words: *The turn of the arms from above downwards*, written against each, to show that the arms move together.

*Fig. 55. First Posture in a Contretemps
de côté à gauche*

Fig. 56. Second Posture in a Contretemps de côté

146   *The* DANCING MASTER

Fig. 57 is to show how the arms should be extended after the hop, and to remind you that the right foot is extended sideways when you hop on the left, as I have explained in Part I; afterwards you close it in the fifth position front and open the left foot to the second position, but during the execution of these steps the arms remain extended without any opposition.

As for the head, when you rise, it should turn slightly towards the side to which you travel, though this is not a fixed rule; for if you dance with someone and make these *contretemps* while passing in front of each other, you must look at each other. So, when I said that the head must be held erect, I did not mean that it should not move, but that it should not be laboured, or held in a strained or affected manner.

CHAPTER XVII

Of the Manner of Moving the Arms with the Contretemps ouvert or Contretemps de Chaconne

THE *contretemps de chaconne* is begun from the third or fourth position, as explained in Part I, therefore it requires opposition; and for this reason, if the left foot be in front, the right arm falls in opposition; and, having the body thus placed and supported on the left foot, you must bend upon it and hop, extending the right arm. Then, open the right foot sideways in the second position, going to the right, and if you close the left foot in the third position back, which is your second step, the left arm simultaneously bends *from below upwards*, which makes the opposition to the right foot in front; but when you close the left foot in the fifth position front, then the right arm makes the opposition. Therefore, there are two different oppositions in this *pas*, which arise from one step, made either *devant* or *derrière*. Hence, at the beginning, the arms must be extended and make no contrast, except

Fig. 57. Third Posture, after the Hop

at the last movement; whereas, in other steps, they are opposed at the beginning.

CHAPTER XVIII

Of the Manner of Moving the Arms with the Contretemps ballonné

THIS *contretemps* is a lively *pas* much used in social dances. The manner of moving the arms is not very difficult, since there is but one opposition required. In truth, there is but one step, but that step contains two movements, as I have said before, which render it sparkling and lively.

If you execute it *en avant*, and have the body supported on the left foot, you bend on it raising the right, and at that moment the right arm turns *from above downwards*, and the left moves *from below upwards*, which makes the opposition to the leg that passes in front; but in alighting on the right for this second movement, the arms must not be changed. You should also observe in this *pas* to keep the body well back, and to turn the head a little towards the arm in opposition.

But when you make this *pas* backwards, you must follow the same rule as in other *pas*, that is, when you step backwards with the right foot, the left arm is in opposition, as it is in front. Thus, when you pass the right foot backwards, you turn the left arm *from above downwards* and return the right *from below upwards*, which induces that change of the arms which should be observed in this *pas*.

As to that made *de côté*, it differs only in that it requires no opposition. For, as its first movement begins from the third or fifth position, and since at the next you fall into the second, which requires no opposition, it is sufficient to make a little movement of the wrists.

These are all the most suitable ways of moving the arms with these *pas*.

CHAPTER XIX

Of the different Manners of Moving the Arms with all Kinds of Chassés

HAVING given you all the simplest ways of executing all kinds of *chassés* in social dances, it is also necessary to explain the method of moving the arms in different ways.

I shall begin with those used in *La Mariée* which, being known all the world over, may be justly termed one of the finest dances ever seen.

These *chassés* occur at the beginning of the third strain, where they are preceded by a *coupé*; therefore, in this *coupé*, you bend both arms and extend them at the first movement of the *chassé*. But at the second, in which you rise on the foot contrary to that which has driven the other, the arm on the side of the rising foot bends, because at the end of this *pas* there is generally a *pas en tournant*; and, as I have already said in the chapter on *pirouettes*, the arm makes it easy for the body to turn on the side to which it is extended, and for this reason this opposition is made. For, if it were as in the *Allemande*, where several are made in succession, there would be no opposition. It is true that there is no movement of the arms in the *chassés* of that dance, because it is quite characteristic.

There is another kind of *chassé* in *L'Aimable Vainqueur*, which is simply a *jeté chassé*, three of which are made in succession and occupy the time of one single *pas*. But one contrast is sufficient for this *pas* which begins at the first movement, and is maintained during the other two *pas*.

They are also made *de côté*, as I have observed in Part I, which contains two plates explanatory of the movements. In this *pas* it is sufficient to have the arms extended. For instance, if you execute it returning to the left side, the right foot should rise to drive the left, therefore the right arm and shoulder should rise more than the left arm and shoulder, though both are extended, because the arms in this *pas* are to aid the balance. Nevertheless, there should be a slight motion of the wrists at the first movement to prevent that stiffness which would otherwise appear.

I have also told you that there are other *chassés*, but since there are none of that kind used in social dances, I shall not discuss the movement of the arms.

CHAPTER XX

Of the Manner of Moving the Arms in Saillies or Pas Echappés

THIS kind of *pas* is peculiar in its manner, and partakes, as it were, of the *pas tombé*, in that you rise *sur les demi-pointes* to begin it. But, as I have shown in Part I how to do it, and since I now have but to teach the movement of the arms, I shall simply state that when you begin, having the feet in the fourth position, and consequently one arm in opposition, that arm must extend *from above downwards*,[1] while the other simultaneously moves *from below upwards*; but no change must be made at the second hop. Afterwards, in making the third, which is an *assemblé*, let both arms fall by your side, then make a slight inclination with your head, and raise it at the same time as your arms when you make another *pas*, for instance, a *pas de bourrée* or such other as the dance requires; for this little movement, when properly made, affords much grace; but beware of affectation.

I have not dealt with the movement of the arms during *tours de jambe* and *ouvertures de jambe*, for in these actions neither the arms nor the body should stir.

There are still other *pas* used in dancing of which I have made no mention, having undertaken in this book to treat solely of the manner of making all the principal *pas* in social dances, and to formulate the simplest methods of performing them with their proper arm movements, to the end that any person may learn to dance with all the good taste and delicacy that this exercise requires, which task I flatter myself I have achieved with success.

[1] During the first movement.